Happy 48th Holmes Family Reunion,

I'm ho[...]
I am happ[y to ...]
provide sch[olarships ...]
in college. Thanks,

[signature]

How to Eradicate Hazing

Ronald W. Holmes, Ph.D.
Publisher, The Holmes Education Post, LLC
"An Education Focused Internet Newspaper"

authorHOUSE®

AuthorHouse™
1663 Liberty Drive
Bloomington, IN 47403
www.authorhouse.com
Phone: 1-800-839-8640

© 2013 Ronald W. Holmes, Ph.D. All rights reserved.

No part of this book may be reproduced, stored in a retrieval system, or transmitted by any means without the written permission of the author.

Published by AuthorHouse 1/8/2013

ISBN: 978-1-4817-0410-6 (sc)
ISBN: 978-1-4817-0408-3 (e)

Library of Congress Control Number: 2013900276

Any people depicted in stock imagery provided by Thinkstock are models, and such images are being used for illustrative purposes only.
Certain stock imagery © Thinkstock.

This book is printed on acid-free paper.

Because of the dynamic nature of the Internet, any web addresses or links contained in this book may have changed since publication and may no longer be valid.

The views expressed in this work are solely those of the author and do not necessarily reflect the views of the publisher, and the publisher hereby disclaims any responsibility for them.

Table of Contents

Introduction	1
Defining Hazing	5
Historical Perspective, Ronald W. Holmes, Ph.D.	6
Psychological Perspective, DeAnna M. Burney, Ph.D.	14
Sociological Perspective, Patricia Warren Hightower, Ph.D.	18
Theological Perspective, Rev. Dr. John H. Grant	21
Legal Perspective, Jarian N. Lyons, Esquire	28
Cultural Perspective, Linda T. Fortenberry, Ph.D.	30
How to Eradicate Hazing	34
Step I - Educate Stakeholders	34
Step II - Review Policies, Procedures and Laws	38
Step III - Address Accountability	41
Step IV - Distinguish Hazing Myths & Truths	47
Step V - Implement Activities	51
Step VI - Communicate Impact	58
Step VII - Advertise using Media	64
Step VIII - Teach Anti-Hazing Curriculum	66
Step IX - Evaluate Strategies	69
Resources	72
References	75
Author's Background	79

ACKNOWLEDGEMENT

In writing this book, "How to Eradicate Hazing," I was inspired by Reverend Dr. R. B. Holmes Jr. in his creating the National Anti-Hazing/Anti-Violence Task Force (NAHAVT) in an effort to eradicate hazing from the culture of historically Black schools and other educational institutions across the nation. Reverend Holmes' initiative was sparked by the tragic death of Florida A&M University (FAMU) drum major, Robert D. Champion Jr. who died on November 19, 2011 due to a hazing ritual from fellow band members.

On Jan. 17, 2012, Holmes launched the National Anti-Hazing/Anti-Violence Task Force in conjunction with the National Save the Family Now Movement, Inc. (NSFNM), the National Newspaper Publishers Association (NNPA) and the National Association for Equal Opportunity in Higher Education (NAFEO) and other groups at the National Press Club in Washington, D.C. The tenor of the message from the task force was that we must make every effort to prevent violence and hazing in our society and especially in our academic institutions.

Mr. and Mrs. Robert Champion Sr., parents of Robert Champion Jr. were present to support the collective efforts of the task force. Members of the task force announced strategies to address hazing and violence across America in general, at historically Black colleges and universities in particular and the K-12 environment. Some members who provided messages included Dr. R.B. Holmes Jr., task force chairman, president of NSFNM and pastor of Bethel Missionary Baptist Church; Dr. George Cooper, task force co-chairman and president of South Carolina State University; attorney Lezli Baskerville, president and chief executive officer of NAFEO and Dr. Ronald Holmes, national superintendent of education of the NSFNM and publisher of The Holmes Education Post, LLC.

For this reason, I would like to thank Reverend Holmes for creating the NAHAVT and inspiring me to write this book as a model to eradicate hazing from American culture. I would also like to thank Dr. DeAnna M. Burney, Dr. Patricia Warren Hightower, Reverend Dr. John H. Grant, attorney Jarian N. Lyons and Dr. Linda T. Fortenberry for providing their articles to support the book.

DEDICATION

We dedicate this book to Mr. & Mrs. Robert Champion Sr. in memory of their son Robert Darnell Champion, Jr. who died tragically. Robert was a drum major in the Marching 100 Band at Florida A&M University. At the age of 26, Robert's life was taken through a hazing ritual of fellow band members after the Florida Classic in Orlando, Florida.

We also dedicate this book to other parents who have lost their loved ones due to hazing and other forms of violence in our schools, universities and communities.

As an advocate for education and humankind, all proceeds of this book will go towards scholarships for the Robert Champion Foundation, Inc. It is our hope that the scholarships will serve as a vehicle to improve public education and encourage the recipients of the scholarships to promote the eradication of hazing in American society.

"TRIBUTE" to Robert D. Champion Jr.

By W Nekole Ross, former band member

On the patch, on the field, leading the parade, doing the things he loved, all while leading the way. Robert had a mission that only he could complete, he lived up to his family name while side stepping all defeat. Prideful, poised, pleasant and kind are just a few terms that come to mind while describing such a wonderful human being. He marched his way into our lives and our hearts with his goals and aspirations all set high. He kept his eye on the prize while never giving up or giving in. He helped those in need and sought to make the world a better place to be. Just as quickly as he marched in with his tasks all plotted out, his mission was complete and God said, "You must now bow out." With tearful eyes and broken hearts, we watched you march away with just as much style and grace as your first performance day. You raised your baton and gave a final bow then faded out of sight but not before leaving the Champion legacy, which we will now honor and take much pride. You taught hard life lessons and some not so easily learned. You will always be beside us to guide us on the right steps, the right turns and the right moves on a difficult life journey. No one could have done it any better, thank God for allowing you to be known. Good night our heroic Champion. Hubba, Hubba Robert! Hubba, Hubba!

FOREWORD

It is critically important that we develop strategies and approaches to eradicate and eliminate hazing from the culture as we know it. The unfortunate and untimely death of Florida A&M University's drum major, Robert Champion on November 19, 2011 has become a wake up call to the nation that hazing is dangerous, demeaning, devastating and deadly. Furthermore, hazing is irresponsible, irrational, immature, illogical and illegal.

The hazing episode that took place at FAMU touched the core of Historically Black Colleges and Universities (HBCU) and administration. Let us be clear, hazing has never been condoned by officials. However, hazing is a dark cultural ritual that has been going on for many years. It must be stated forthrightly that hazing is not a Black problem or a Black band problem. Hazing is a challenge and we must do all we can to weed it out of our culture.

The National Anti-Hazing/Anti-Violence Task Force was organized to motivate and mobilize major stakeholders to work collectively to purge hazing from our culture. The task force developed a three year strategic plan that if executed, will lead to the eradication of hazing. Our plan of action is included in this book. We must address the psychological, sociological and theological ramification for the cause and cure of hazing! If we don't consistently and persistently address this problem, it will damage greatly the prestige and greatness of HBCU's and other educational institutions.

FAMU is not the only institution, Black or White, that has been torn because of hazing. FAMU has become the focal point because of its revered and famous band, the renowed Marching 100. FAMU will rise again and can use this tragedy to change the culture of hazing! However, FAMU can't solve this problem alone. It will take the general public to make it clear that hazing is unacceptable. We are calling the

Black press, churches, elected officials, educators, parents and students to stand up against any group or person who insists on hazing.

The time is now for all of us to become actively involved to tackle the problem and pain of violence on Black college campuses, Black community and other communities. I hope that this book will inspire and challenge us to do our level best to rid, purge and root out hazing from our culture. Make no mistake about hazing, it didn't begin with Robert Champion, but prayerfully, it must end with the death of our drum major and other beloved children throughout the country. Let's become a champion in this fight!

Reverend Dr. R. B. Holmes Jr.
Pastor of Bethel Missionary Baptist Church
President/CEO, Live Communications
Founder/Chair, National Anti-Hazing/Anti-Violence Task Force

Introduction

Hazing is an epidemic in the American culture. It occurs in various facets of our American culture including the military, sports, workplace and education. According to Hoover (1999), hazing is defined as "any activity expected of someone to join a group that has the potential to humiliate, degrade, abuse or endanger a person regardless of his or her willingness to participate" in the activity. The activity is normally affiliated with an individual being physically and psychologically abused, depriving of sleep, carrying unwarranted objects, consuming alcohol, participating in sexual acts and paddling (Nuwer cited in Chang 2011). Hazing activity is typically enacted during a period of time (Keaton et al., cited in Chang 2011). Hazing activity can occur on or off campus of educational institutions, by an individual alone or acting with others for the purpose of pledging, being initiated into, affiliating with holding office in an organization or maintaining membership in an organization.

In a national study on student hazing at the University of Maine consisting of 11,482 undergraduate students from 53 colleges and universities, 55 percent of college students affiliated with groups, organizations and teams experienced some type of hazing. In about 95 percent of the hazing incidents, students did not report their cases to the campus officials. Half of these hazing

> Hazing has the potential to abuse or endanger a person.

incidents are placed on the internet by the offending group (Allan and Madden 2008).

Joining groups, organizations and teams are about gaining acceptance, belonging and affection as a part of students' social needs. Students willingly or unwillingly participate in hazing activity to gain membership in an organization. According to the National Collegiate Athletic Association (NCAA), "many student-athletes believe the myths that hazing will accomplish team building and bonding, instill needed humility in new team members, establish a hierarchy for leadership and decision-making within the team, allow individuals free choice regarding their participation and be fun and harmless."

Similar to the university level, hazing is prevalent in the K-12 environment. According to the findings from a national study at Alfred University of 1500 students from a random sample of 20,000 high school students, 48 percent reported being hazed, 30 percent participated in potential illegal acts and 25 percent noted being hazed before the age of 13. Moreover, students reported participating in hazing because it enabled them to feel closer as a group, provided approval by their peers and afforded an opportunity for revenge. Other students took part in hazing rituals because they were ill-informed, uneducated, pressured and influenced by the culture of the environment including the convictions of adults.

The effects of hazing may impact students emotionally and physically causing them to perform poorly in school, start a fight, participate in a crime, get injured, commit suicide or lose a life. Despite the adoption of laws in 44 states prohibiting hazing in our educational settings, there were three deaths in 2011 including students at Florida A&M University, Cornell University and University of Northern Colorado. There were also four deaths in 2012 at Vincennes University, Fresno State University, Madison High School in Madison, North Dakota, and Northern Illinois University (Nuwer, 2012). Just as the hazing incidents are steadily occuring, educational institutions are increasingly faced with legal challenges regarding these fatalities. At the same time, courts are bombarded with legal cases and decisions to determine if there was a "duty of care" between the hazing victims and educational institutions.

To eliminate the myths of hazing on college and university campuses, the NCAA recommends that higher education administrators employ comprehensive strategies for hazing preventions at all levels (individual, institution, group, community and public policy). They recommend that schools clearly define the consequences for documented hazing occurrences and establish an effective method for investigating allegations of hazing incidents. Finally, schools should assure legal steps are followed in line with allegations of hazing incidents.

Similarly, the findings of the national study on student hazing at the University of Maine and Alfred University recommend that higher education administrators make hazing prevention inclusive to all student groups on campus and that they extensively educate all stakeholders of the campus community about the seriousness and dangers of hazing. The study also recommends that schools create hazing interventions that are researched-centered and evaluate them periodically to measure their effectiveness for hazing preventions.

With these interventions applying to secondary settings as well, it is time for change. It is time to eradicate hazing from American culture. We know that change can happen. In 2011, we saw individuals and groups advocating for change of the U.S. culture through Occupy Wall Street. In the same year, we saw individuals and groups in the Middle East and North Africa advocating for change of civil unrest through various protest methods. Therefore, this book discusses a nine-step model to eradicate hazing from the American culture including an evaluation component. Using the acronyms from the word "Eradicate," this book provides a model (See figure 1) for better understanding and reinforcement of the strategies to end hazing once and for all.

(Figure 1)

ERADICATE	Nine-Step Model
E	Educate all stakeholders on policies, procedures and laws on hazing.
R	Review routinely policies, procedures and laws on hazing.
A	Address and ensure all stakeholders are accountable to policies, procedure and laws on hazing.
D	Distinguish hazing myths and truths.
I	Implement activities in educational setting and community on anti-hazing prevention strategies.
C	Communicate the impact of hazing on victims and their families, as well as their solutions to end it.
A	Advertise continuously in the media researched-based solutions and best practices on eradicating hazing.
T	Teach anti-hazing curriculum in educational setting and community.
E	Evaluate periodically anti-hazing prevention strategies in educational setting and community.

Defining Hazing

With hazing being interwoven in American society and constantly occurring at the secondary and postsecondary levels, we must clearly understand the meaning of hazing from a historical, psychological, sociological, theological, legal and cultural perspective.

Historical Perspective, Ronald W. Holmes, Ph.D.

Hazing is defined as "any activity expected of someone to join a group that has the potential to humiliate, degrade, abuse or endanger a person regardless of his or her willingness to participate" in the activity (Hoover, 1999). Some examples of hazing include paddling or beating a person, depriving a person of sufficient sleep, requiring or encouraging an individual to consume alcohol, drugs or unusual substances, kidnapping or confining an individual and subjecting a person to cruel and unusual psychological conditions (Alfred University, 2012).

According to the National Collegiate Athletic Association (2007), "many student-athletes believe the myths that hazing will accomplish team building and bonding, instill needed humility in new team members, establish a hierarchy for leadership and decision-making within the team, allow individuals free choice regarding their participation and be fun and harmless." The fact is that hazing has the potential to degrade, humiliate, abuse or endanger an individual through acts of their perpetrators while participating in a group willingly or unwillingly.

Hazing is not new to our society. It was first documented by Greek philosopher Plato in 387 B.C. and by a group known as "Overturners" in the fourth century at the Center of Learning in Carthage according to Nuwer cited in Ellsworth (2004). Through other periods of society, hazing was documented during the middle ages of students at medieval universities and in the U.S. at Harvard College in 1657. The first two hazing deaths were documented in higher education at Franklin Seminary (Kentucky) in 1838 and Amherst College (Massachusetts) in 1847. The first known fraternity-associated hazing death was at Cornell University in 1873, which involved a student being blindfolded and tumbled into a gorge. The first reported college athlete-associated hazing was in 1923 at Hobart College, which involved a freshman being beaten and thrown into a lake. Figure 2 provides a chronology of U.S. hazing deaths according to Nuwer (2012).

While participation in hazing occurs in various extra-curricular activities (athletics, sororities, fraternities, etc.) it was initially documented in the marching band in the early 20th century according to Nuwer cited in Ellsworth (2004). This included the University of Gettyburg where a group of sophomores hazed freshman members of the marching band, as well as similar occurrences at Columbia and Barnard Colleges. Other documented cases of hazing incidents included in 1981 where an associate band director at FAMU tried to eradicate hazing when a 17 year old band member was beaten; in 1984 where a band fraternity, Kappa Kappa Psi, at the University of Akron was charged with hazing and in 1984 where a band director at the University of Southern California reported encouraging upperclassmen to haze incoming band members.

Additionally, a marching band student leader and another member at Florida State University were removed permanently from the band due to a hazing incident. In August and September 2012 respectively, Clark Atlanta and Texas Southern Universities' marching bands were suspended for possible allegations of hazing. On the secondary level, DeKalb County School System in December 2011 suspended their entire student marching band activities at 19 schools to investigate allegations of "inappropriate behavior" in the marching band programs. The investigation started after several of FAMU's students, who were graduates of DeKalb County, were either victimized of hazing activities at the university or charged for participating in hazing activities.

As noted, hazing allegations, incidents and/or deaths are steadily occurring, and educational institutions are increasingly faced with legal challenges regarding these fatalities. At the same time, courts are bombarded with legal cases and decisions to determine if institutions have a "duty of care" or "duty to protect" hazing victims. For example, the hazing incident in 1993 at the University of Nebraska, the Nebraska Supreme Court ruled that the university had a duty to protect a fraternity pledge who was severely injured (brain-damaged) while trying to escape fraternity members who were hazing him on the university property.

> Hazing examples include paddling, beating and kidnapping.

Specifically, this hazing incident involved several fraternity members confronting the pledge victim in the basement of the institution's building, tackled and handcuffed him to a another member, radiator and toilet pipe on separate occasions and forced him to drink excessive alcohol. After becoming ill, the pledge victim broke free from the toilet pipe, attempted to escape through a bathroom window, fell and, subsequently, encountered severe brain damage. The court noted the institution was aware of previous criminal conducts such as sexual assault and theft involving members of fraternities on the campus. The court further stated the institution was obligated "to take reasonable steps to protect against acts of hazing, including student abduction on the university's property and the harm that naturally flows therefrom" (Reisberg, 1999).

In 1874, the first anti-hazing statue was established in the U.S. This was the result of humiliation new Navy men were experiencing in the Naval Academy (Gayadeen, 2011). Twenty-seven years later, Illinois adopted the first anti-hazing law in 1901. Even with the enactment of anti-hazing laws in 44 states (See figure 3), there appears to be some disparities between the laws in one state versus another. For example, the state of Maryland only recognizes physical hazing whereas the state of Florida recognizes physical and psychological hazing (Ellsworth, 2004).

(Figure 2)
List of U.S. Schools with Hazing Deaths

Schools	# of Deaths	Year (s)
Alcorn State University	1	1993
Alfred University	2	1978, 2002
American International College	1	1984
Amherst College	1	1847
Auburn University	1	1993
Baylor University	1	1967
Bloomsburg University	1	1994
Bluefield State College	1	1974
Bradley University	1	2003

Schools	# of Deaths	Year (s)
Brown University	1	1949
California State University (Chico)	1	1984
California State University (Los Angeles)	2	2002, 2002
Cal Poly	1	2008
Chico State University	2	2000, 2005
Clarkson University (New York)	1	1980
Clarkson University & State University of New York at Potsdam	1	1997
Cheyney University of Pennsylvania	1	1975
Colgate University	1	1919
College of the City of New York	1	1917
Cornell University	3	1894, 1899, 2011
Cornell University (New York)	1	1873
Dickinson College	1	1990
Eastern Illinois University	1	1970
Ferris State University	1	1999
Florida A&M University	1	2011
Franklin and Marshall College (Pennsylvania)	1	1923
Franklin Seminary (Kentucky)	1	1838
Fresno State University	1	2012
Frostburg State University	1	1992
Georgetown College (Kentucky)	1	1965
Grove City College (Pennsylvania)	4	1974, 1974, 1974, 1974
Hamilton College (New York)	1	1922
Indiana University	2	1929, 2001
Iona College (New York)	1	1999
Ithaca College	1	1980
Kenyon College (Ohio)	1	1905
Lamar University (Texas)	1	1986

Ronald W. Holmes, Ph.D.

Schools	# of Deaths	Year (s)
Lawrenceville High School (New Jersey)	1	1899
Lehigh University (Pennsylvania)	1	1973
Lenoir Rhyne	1	2008
Loras College (Iowa)	1	1978
Louisiana State University	2	1979, 1997
Madison High School (Madison, North Dakota)	1	2012
Massachusetts Institute of Technology	3	1900, 1956, 1997
Mississippi State University	1	1980
Monmouth College (New Jersey)	1	1974
Morehouse College	1	1989
New Mexico Military Institute	1	1915
North Carolina Central University	1	1977
North Carolina State University	1	1997
Northern Illinois University	2	1975, 2012
Northwestern University (Illinois)	2	1921, 1923
Pierce College (California)	1	1972
Plattsburgh State (State University of New York)	1	2003
Plymouth State University	1	2003
Prairie View A&M University	1	2009
Purdue University (Indiana)	1	1913
Radford University	1	2010
Rider College (New Jersey)	1	1988
Rider University	1	2007
Rochester Institute of Technology	1	2003
Rutgers University	2	1979, 1988
San Diego State University	2	2002, 2002
Southeast Missouri State	1	1994
Stanford University	1	1987

How to Eradicate Hazing

Schools	# of Deaths	Year (s)
State University of New York at Albany	1	1988
St. John's Military College	1	1914
St. John's University (New York)	1	1976
St. Louis University (Missouri)	1	1945
SUNY Geneseo	1	2009
Swarthmore College (Pennsylvania)	1	1954
Tennessee State University	2	1983, 2001
Texas A&M University	2	1984, 1997
Texas Tech University	1	1976
Trinity University (Texas)	1	1991
Towson State University	1	1982
Tulane University	1	1971
University of California, Los Angeles (UCLA)	2	1997, 1997
United States Military Academy (New York)	1	1900
University of Alabama	1	1923
University of Arkansas	1	1987
University of California (Berkeley)	2	1950, 1991
University of California (Davis)	1	1984
University of California (Irvine)	1	2005
University of California (Santa Barbara)	1	1957
University of Colorado	2	1985, 2004
University of Delaware	1	2008
University of Georgia	1	2000
University of Kentucky	1	1915
University of Lowell (Massachusetts)	1	1980
University of Maryland	2	1972, 2002
University of Maryland (Baltimore)	1	1903
University of Miami	1	2001
University of Michigan	1	1998

Schools	# of Deaths	Year (s)
University of Minnesota (Duluth)	1	2001
University of Mississippi	2	1987, 1998
University of Missouri	2	1940, 1980
University of Missouri (Rolla)	2	1977, 1991
University of Missouri (Columbia)	1	1985
University of Nevada (Reno)	2	1975, 2002
University of North Carolina	1	1912
University of North Dakota	1	1980
University of Northern Colorado	1	2011
University of Oklahoma	1	2004
University of Pennsylvania	1	1977
University of Richmond	2	1988, 1999
University of South Carolina	1	1980
University of Southern California	1	1959
University of Texas 2005, 2006	7	1928, 1986, 1988,1995, 1998
University of Vermont	1	1992
University of Virginia	4	1982, 1982, 1992, 1996
University of Washington	1	1998
University of Wisconsin (Steven Point)	1	1975
University of Wisconsin (Superior)	1	1981
Utah State	1	2008
Vincennes University	1	2012
Virginia State College	2	1979, 1979
Wabash College	1	2008
Washington State University	1	1975
Western Illinois University	1	1990
Wittenberg University (Ohio)	1	1950
Worcester Polytechnic Institute	1	1908
Yale University	5	1892, 2003, 2003, 2003, 2003

How to Eradicate Hazing

(Figure 3)

Anti-Hazing Laws in U.S. States

State / Enactment Date		
• Illinois 1901	• Pennsylvania 1986	• Tennessee 1995
• Rhode Island 1909	• Missouri 1987	• Texas 1995
• North Carolina 1913	• South Carolina 1987	• West Virginia 1995
• Louisiana 1920	• Connecticut 1988	• Minnesota 1997
• Michigan 1931	• Georgia 1988	• Colorado 1999
• Virginia 1975	• Iowa 1989	• Nevada 1999
• California 1976	• Maine 1989	• Vermont 1999
• Indiana 1976	• Utah 1989	• Arizona 2001
• New Jersey 1980	• Mississippi 1990	• Florida 2002
• Alabama 1981	• Oklahoma 1990	• Maryland 2002
• Ohio 1982	• Idaho 1991	***States with Non-Anti-Hazing Laws:***
• Arkansas 1983	• Delaware 1992	• Alaska
• New York 1983	• New Hampshire 1993	• Hawaii
• Oregon 1983	• Washington (State) 1993	• Montana
• Wisconsin 1983	• Nebraska 1994	• New Mexico
• Massachusetts 1985	• North Dakota 1995	• South Dakota
• Kansas 1986		• Wyoming
• Kentucky 1986		

Psychological Perspective, DeAnna M. Burney, Ph.D.

"When our own thoughts are forbidden, when our questions are not allowed and our doubts are punished, when contacts and friendships outside the organization are censored, we are being abused for an end that never justifies the means. If there is any lesson to be learned, it is that an ideal can never be brought about by fear, abuse and the threat of retribution. When family and friends, and associates are used as a weapon in order to force us to stay in an organization, something has gone terribly wrong."

The words spoken by Deborah Layton are a warning that the importance of the organization should never become more important than the value of human life. While Layton was a survivor of abuse within an organization, Robert Champion was not. Mr. Champion's death sends a clear message that something within a system and organization has gone terribly wrong. Harassment, beatings, defamation, unequal forms of treatment and homicides are outcomes of social oppression that has become ingrained within the social structure of many organizations.

The question is, why does hazing continue? What are the causes? What are the treatments for eradication and elimination? First, hazing continues because it is protected and accepted as an institutional process that gives individuals the right for privileged entry. Beyond established hierarchies in relationships, the primary goal of hazing is to create a system of rank based on domination and oppression that forms power and control over the organization and those who are perceived as less relevant in the organization. There are three reasons why this socially oppressive behavior continues within the adolescent culture:

1. Hazing is about protecting power and control—the power dynamic plays a significant role in the maintenance of hazing. Those who are perceived to be or who are actually in positions of power in organizations use verbal, physical and psychological

threats and punishments to control the thinking and behavior of those who are perceived as less powerful.
2. Hazing is about protecting a reign of error—the desire of those who are younger or in less powerful positions in the organization are driven to "consent" by word or deed to hazing activities. Once they have survived their period of hazing, they have the opportunity to then carry on the tradition of hazing with the next generation. "They do what was done to them." The status quo or the reign of error is effectively protected and carried forward from one generation to the next.
3. Hazing is about protecting a socialized process through a code of silence. The code is simply not to tell what happened during the hazing process. It is believed that uniform silence protects all members if caught in the act of hazing. Unfortunately, the motivation to consciously maintain a code of silence protects the organization, not the members of the organization. The "code of silence" maintains and legitimizes hazing as a normal and acceptable act within an organization. As a result, hazing is imbedded and conditioned in the psyche and behavior of those within an organization, and thus becomes an institutionalized behavior that is protected and accepted as normal practice.

Beyond protecting a code of silence, hazing can only occur when there is an environment and time to conduct the act of hazing. Like criminals, hazers and bystanders seek ungoverned environments and time to perform uncensored opportunities to haze their victims. Yes, persons who are hazed are victims of the hazer. Both psychologists and criminologists agree that antisocial behaviors are conducted by persons who have minimal regard for others and social rules. These individuals may have a history of persistent lying or deceit, use charm to manipulate others, difficulty with

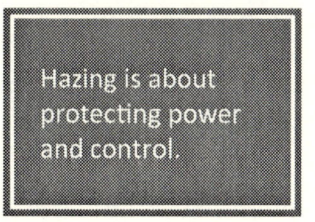

> Hazing is about protecting power and control.

the law, history of violating the rights of others, intimidation, aggressive or violent behavior, display anger and agitation, as well as poor or abusive relationships. While hazers, bystanders, and the hazed understand that hazing is illegal, these behaviors continue without regret and remorse for their actions toward their victims. The intensity of antisocial symptoms tends to peak during the 20's (the point of post adolescents and during college life and then may decrease over time). Thus, it must be understood that hazing is a socialized behavioral condition that is expressed during a period of adolescence or when a mature adult regresses back into an adolescent state.

Acceptance into college life will often mask antisocial behaviors and other hidden mental health disabilities. In 2007, 18- to 25-year-olds have one of the highest rates of severe psychological distress out of any age group, and also have the lowest rate of seeking help, according to the Substance Abuse and Mental Health Services Administration (SAMHSA). In a 2007 report by the National Institute of Mental Health (NIMH), each year one of four college students suffers from some diagnosable mental disorder. These disorders are caused by many conditions that result in relationship problems. Because these students are "unknown and their mental health issues and behaviors are masked, it is not until they began to engage in antisocial behaviors that the victims, bystanders, and advisors of these organizations recognize that the excessive violence and abuse by the unknown student hazer is perhaps more than hazing and rites of passage, but perhaps psychological aggressive punishment misplaced on the hazee. Ninety percent of counseling centers have reported a rise in students with severe psychological distress, according to a 2005 report by Gallagher and Graham.

Thus, within university systems, we can no longer ignore the history of students entering college campuses and those who seek membership within student led organizations. Consideration must be given to the social and environmental experiences that students have lived prior to enrolling into college. Examination of their background and mental health status prior to seeking membership in any student organization should be explored. This analysis suggests that the eradication and elimination of hazing must involve a treatment process that is systemically multidimensional, multifaceted, and multicultural in focus. That is, there must be a cultural focus of the student population that is being reviewed due to hazing. Can eradication be achieved? Over time and with consistency of method, both eradication and elimination can be obtained.

Dr. DeAnna M. Burney is a psychology professor at Florida A&M University. As part of the National Anti-Hazing/Anti-Violence Task Force's initiative to address, "The Culture, Cause and Cure for Hazing," this article first appeared in the Capital Outlook Newspaper on March 19, 2012 entitled, "Psychological solutions for the elimination of hazing."

Sociological Perspective, Patricia Warren Hightower, Ph.D.

In the United States, hazing has increasingly become a problem in high schools, fraternities and sororities, athletic teams, and other professional organizations. Although there are a variety of scholarly definitions of hazing, for our purposes it is defined as individuals being forced to commit an act or acts in order to be initiated into or affiliated with a particular organization. Such events include but are not limited to, alcohol binge drinking, blood pinning, sexual assaults, drowning and psychological abuse.

In the US, the first-known hazing incident dates back to 1657 when Harvard University administrators fined several upperclassmen for hazing freshman students. Since that time, there have been other known fatal hazing incidences on college campuses which have led to student deaths at the University of Texas, University of Maryland, Auburn University and many other academic institutions. As a result, by 2011, 44 states have passed anti-hazing legislation with the purpose of criminalizing individuals that engage in such acts while also sending a "zero tolerance" message.

Despite the large social movement surrounding hazing, one question continues to plague us is: Why does hazing continue to exist? According to Hank Nuwer, several factors must be considered in order to understand the ongoing existence of hazing: First, as an American culture, we have not and do not publicly denounce it. In fact, Nuwer notes that a fairly large percentage of the U.S. population defends hazing as a necessary and important ritual. In one of Nuwer's studies, he found that several respondents openly accepted hazing as a "rites of passage" into certain clubs and organizations." For example, one respondent stated that "America is the home of the free and if he wants to join organizations that beat the crap out of them, then he should be allowed to." Another notable respondent, who is also a mother stated, "There are so many wimps in U.S. society. Everybody wants to be a victim. Hazing among athletic teams, and other social groups, is a rewarding and bonding experience." These kinds of philosophical stances reinforce the culture of acceptance of hazing and until we publicly denounce it as a larger societal problem, it will continue to exist.

Next, we currently view hazing as an individual problem that only affects a few people. This approach is problematic because it does not view hazing as a systemic problem. That is, hazing is a national epidemic that crosses racial, ethnic, class and university boundaries. High school and college administrators must be encouraged to create anti-hazing policies, just like they have adopted anti-bullying strategies. The policies must clearly define hazing and outline how they will punish those individuals who are caught engaging in such acts. Without such efforts, hazing will continue.

Finally, it is still unclear why our children and young adults allow themselves to be hazed. In order to more fully understand the realities surrounding hazing, we must accept the fact that we have generations of students who are "Dying to belong." That is, they are so eager to associate themselves with a particular organization that they are willing to be beaten, kicked, slapped, drowned in alcohol and sexually assaulted all for the purposes of "belonging." We must teach our children and young adults that brotherhood and sisterhood is not connected to abuse. Bullying does not signify love. We do not tell the domestic violence victim that they are being loved when they are being smacked around or verbally assaulted. Instead, we encourage them to get far away from their abuser as quickly as they can. So, we must instill the same value in our children. We must also discourage the culture of silence that is associated with the need to belong. Students must have a safe haven to report such abuse without fear of backlash from their peers and other organization affiliates.

> As an American culture, we have not publicly denounced hazing.

These factors in combination will not solve the problem of hazing quickly. Nor are these ideas intended to point the finger or blame any individual or academic institution. Rather, the points expressed here should be used to call attention to the mechanisms that have given

Ronald W. Holmes, Ph.D.

rise to a culture of hazing that is detrimentally affecting our young people.

Dr. Patricia Warren Hightower is an associate professor and director of Undergraduate Studies in the College of Criminology and Criminal Justice at Florida State University. As part of the National Anti-Hazing/Anti-Violence Task Force's initiative to address, "The Culture, Cause and Cure for Hazing," this article first appeared in the Capital Outlook Newspaper on February 17, 2012 entitled, "The sociological lens and the problem of hazing."

Theological Perspective, Rev. Dr. John H. Grant

The research[1] reveals some disturbing facts about the nature and pervasiveness of hazing:

- Hazing is any activity expected of someone joining or participating in a group that has potential to humiliate, degrade, abuse, or endanger a person regardless of that person's willingness to participate. Its danger is compounded by the fact that it is frequently dismissed or minimized as harmless pranks.
- There is substantial evidence of pervasive and persistent hazing and its negative consequences in middle school, high school, colleges and universities, as well as in community organizations, the military and sports at nearly all levels.
- Hazing is an impediment to positive educational climates in schools at all levels. Recently, a local mortician said to me that the year he pledged to a fraternity, and the consequent hazing experience, resulted in the lowest grades and worse academic year of his college career.
- Hazing is often abusive and violent behavior that threatens the health and safety of those hazed. It commonly involves alcohol consumption, humiliation, isolation, sleep deprivation, sex acts, sexual abuse, and other unsafe activities. Emotional and physical harm, including death, are well-documented outcomes.

Metaphors familiar to the Christian community are those that describe Christians, followers of Jesus Christ, as the salt of the earth and the light of the world (Matthew 5:13-16). These illustrate how the Christian community is to impact the larger culture. Salt is a preservative. Light reveals and functions to show the way. As salt, the Christian community can be powerful in the promotion and preservation of values that affirm and respect the inherent dignity and worth of all human personality

---

1 See hazingstudy.org, HazingPrevention.org, and StopHazing.org.

– values that are violated by the viciousness of hazing. The Christian community can also act as light shining on, exposing and educating about, the devastating effects of hazing and why it must not be tolerated in courteous and civilized culture.

Other biblical metaphors that speak to the issue of hazing include those of God as love, God as light, and God as the source and giver of life (1 John 4:8; 1 John 1:5; John 1:4). The words "God is love" describe God's nature as unselfish and unlimited in the extent to which God acts in behalf of the well-being of others. This speaks of God's mercy and compassion which fail not (Lamentations 3:22).

The words "God is light" (1 John 1:5) describe God's nature as pure and without any darkness at all, a nature darkness cannot overcome (John 1:5). "Works of darkness" are any works which oppose God or transgress the word, way, and will of God.

The words "in God is life" (John 1:4) signify the sacredness of human life in particular and all life in general. Any abuse of life is also an abuse of God as the life-giving source, and such abuse is to be roundly resisted, exposed, and condemned.

The metaphors mentioned offer direction for what ought to be our disposition and position on hazing. As people of God, we are called to be salt by manifesting His love, reflecting His light, and embodying His life. The parameters of this present article limit the remainder of our discussion to the metaphor of God as love and some of love's theological and practical implications for hazing.

> *Then one of them, a lawyer, asked Him a question, testing Him, and saying, "Teacher, which is the great commandment in the law?" Jesus said to him, "You shall love the Lord your God with all your heart, with all your soul, and with all your mind.' This is the first and great commandment. And the second is like it: 'You shall love your neighbor as yourself.' On these two commandments hang all the Law and the Prophets." (Matthew 22:35-40, NKJV)*

Jesus teaches in the above passages that the two greatest commandments are to love God and love our neighbor as ourselves. Dr. Martin Luther King, Jr. referred to the content of these two great commandments as a coherent triangle which describes life at its best. This triangle describes what he called "the length, breadth, and height of life." The length of life is the inward drive to achieve one's personal ends and ambitions, an inward concern for one's own welfare and achievements. The breadth of life is the outward concern for the welfare of others. The height of life is the upward reach for God. At the top of the triangle is the Infinite Person, God. At one angle are other persons. At the other angle is the individual person, yourself.

Godly love of self comes from knowing at least two things:

1. That you are the creation of God. Created in God's image does not mean physical image, but refers to God-like moral and spiritual attributes. Persons created in God's image are endowed with the highest dignity and honor and are to be treated as such. Disrespecting or dishonoring anyone is unacceptable, and for one to accept dishonor and disrespect is to fail to respect, love and honor oneself.
2. That you are the actual object of God's love, which is the greatest and most supreme love of all. Because you are the object of the most supreme love from the most supreme Being, you are a creature upon whom God has placed the most infinite value and worth. When you allow anyone to treat you otherwise, you deny your own dignity and worth and fail to properly love yourself.

Hazing profanes all three angles of the triangle and contributes to an incoherent life. It disregards God, disparages others, and accepts disrespect for oneself – when one allows oneself to be hazed. Such a profane violation of the dignity of human personhood cries out for a response from the faith community. The basis of this response is found not so much in the Great Commission to go into all the world and make disciples (Matthew 28:18-20) as in the Great Commandment to love God and to "love your neighbor as yourself."

Ronald W. Holmes, Ph.D.

To paraphrase John Stott:

> *Here are the two instructions of Jesus — a great commandment, "love your neighbor" and a great commission, "go and make disciples." What is the relation between the two? Some of us behave as if we thought them identical, so that if we share the gospel with a person, we consider we have completed our responsibility to love that person. But no . . . God created persons who are my neighbors. . . . Therefore, if we love our neighbors as God made them, we must inevitably be concerned for their total welfare, the good of their souls, their bodies and their communities.*[2]

Our "neighbor" is anyone to whom we can show mercy and compassion (Luke 10:36-37). Hazing demonstrates a lack of compassion for the total welfare of our neighbors, a lack of compassion for the good of their souls, as well as for the good of their bodies and communities. We must not be a part of denying the mercy and compassion to neighbors that we would not want denied to ourselves. We are not to impose on neighbors and their families what we would not want imposed on us and our families. This is what it means to love your neighbor as yourself.

The task of the Christian church is to share and proclaim the gospel of Jesus Christ for the purpose of making disciples (followers of Christ) of our neighbors (Matthew 28:18-20). Rightly understood, the gospel is holistic. It addresses and responds to the needs of the whole person. Luke 4:18ff, as well as numerous other passages throughout the Bible, makes clear that God's will is for all persons to be delivered from anything or anyone that would oppress or abuse them. The gospel does not single out "spiritual" needs and speak only to those; neither does it single out "social" or "physical" needs and speaks only to those. It speaks to the total needs of persons.

The gospel is concerned with deliverance from personal sin and corporate or institutional sin. The church's mandate is to move beyond merely calling individuals to repentance to calling corporations and institutions

---

2 John R. W. Stott, *Christian Mission in the Modern World* (Downers Grove, ILL.: Inter-Varsity Press, 1975), 30.

to repentance. Corporations and institutions whose practices, as opposed to their official policies, tacitly permit such things as hazing are to be called to accountability. The church is to see worship not only as an encounter with God in the sanctuary, but also as a call and challenge to get involved in and improve the quality of community life, both individually and collectively. Worship in the sanctuary without work in the community is unacceptable. Tithes and offerings without trust and obedience are unacceptable. Hymns without holiness are unacceptable. Evangelistic rhetoric which ignores economic realities is unacceptable. And concerns about holiness should not be divorced from concerns about hazing.

Personal piety and holiness do not mean forfeiting our citizenship rights to participate in shaping public and institutional policies that impact the well-being of persons. From the standpoint of citizenship rights and responsibilities, individual Christian believers have the same rights as any other Americans to influence culture by voting and promoting their values. We should not allow others to relegate Christian views and values to the four walls of church buildings, while anti- or non-Christian views and values are proliferated throughout the culture. When Christians withdraw from the public or political arenas, or otherwise allow non-Christians to intimidate them into silence, then the holiness and righteousness which they represent are not reflected in those arenas.

This emphasis on impacting the social and political arenas is firmly rooted in our Judeo-Christian heritage. In his book, *Stride Toward Freedom,* Dr. Martin Luther King Jr. says:

> *Any religion that professes to be concerned with the souls of men and is not concerned with the slums that damn them, the economic conditions that strangle them, and the social conditions that cripple them is a dry-as-dust religion. Such religion is the kind the Marxists like to see — an opiate of the people.*[3]

It is a religion devoid of love. To ensure that ours is not a dry-as-dust

---

3   Martin Luther King, Jr., (Harper & Brothers, 1958), 36.

religion, what are some specific, concrete and practical actions that may be taken either individually by Christians or collectively by the Christian community to address hazing? The Reverend Doctor R. B. Holmes, President of the National Save the Family Now movement, has shared a 12 Point Plan of Action.[4] The Plan mirrors our collective belief that the faith community is responsible for the well-being of others, should not remain silent, can make a difference, and must take action to impact and transform the culture of hazing.

Dr. Latta R. Thomas is one of my former professors at Benedict College in Columbia, South Carolina, to whom I own a great debt of gratitude for the way he helped change the direction of my life! In his book, *The Biblical God and Human Suffering*, Dr. Thomas observes rightly and insightfully that:

> *The biblical God adamantly abhors, divinely detests and uncompromisingly undermines the forces that make for human suffering. Agony and misery in the human ranks impugn both God's sovereignty and compassion; therefore, God is making the elimination of such suffering a priority action which he will not abandon. . . . A just and compassionate God fighting against human misery in this world is the consistent and continuous theme throughout the Old Testament and New Testament. This central emphasis is always seen rising above any sub-themes.*[5]

This truth is also echoed in one of America's foundational documents, the Declaration of Independence, adopted in 1776:

> *We hold these truths to be self-evident, that <u>all men are created equal</u>, that they are endowed by their Creator with certain unalienable rights, that among these are <u>life, liberty and the pursuit of happiness</u>.*

Hazing violates each of these unalienable rights. It violates life by dehumanizing it. It violates liberty by depriving a person of it – even if

---

4 The Plan may be viewed at www.savethefamilynow.com.

5 Latta R. Thomas, (David C. Cook Publishing Co., 1987), 14 and 38.

that deprivation is only for a designated "pledge period" of time. It violates the pursuit of happiness by disrupting and scaring it. It relegates the precious personhood of human beings to something to be disrespected, demeaned, degraded, damaged, and even destroyed via death. The Christian community, inclusive of the Black pulpit and the Black press, can have a greater impact on the elimination of hazing by publicly and openly speaking up against and exposing it. Obviously, if we remain silent, our voices will not be heard, and our silence may be regarded as sanction!

> Hazing demonstrates a lack of compassion for the total welfare of our neighbors and ourselves.

Rev. Dr. John H. Grant is pastor and president of the Mt. Zion Missionary Baptist Church of Asheville, Inc. and vice president of the National Save the Family Now Movement, Inc. He presented part of this theological perspective at conferences of the National Anti-Hazing/Anti-Violence Task Force and National Newspaper Publishers Association in South Carolina and Virginia respectively.

Legal Perspective, Jarian N. Lyons, Esquire

Long before the untimely and tragic death of Robert Champion, the Florida Legislature already determined that hazing was a crime. Nonetheless, hazing has been a trend that has plagued our society for generations. What has been lost with the recent events of hazing is that hazing is bigger than Florida A&M University. In fact, 44 of our 50 states have laws prohibiting hazing, which speak volumes regarding the seriousness of this epidemic. Likewise, countries such as the Philippines, Russia and Indonesia have laws against hazing. Nonetheless, hazing still occurs in an alarming fashion despite the attendant consequences of serious injury, death or prison. In Florida, a person accused of committing an act of hazing faces a sentence of up to five years in prison along with a $5,000 fine. What's lost in situations involving hazing is that it takes two. In other words, hazing is a choice.

Though traditions often compel an individual to adhere to an organization's practices, a line should be drawn between tradition and crime. Arguably, one seeking membership into an organization or group doesn't have a choice if they want to become a member. On the contrary, both the actor and the receiver of hazing can choose to abstain from participating.

The problem in most cases of hazing is that neither the actor nor the victim knows when to draw the line. Looking deeper into how Florida defines hazing stretches the matter beyond physical contact. Florida Statute 1006.63 defines hazing as pressuring or coercing a person into violating state or federal law, any brutality of a physical nature, such as whipping, beating, branding, exposure to the elements, forced consumption of any food, liquor, drug or other substance, or other forced physical activity that could adversely affect one's physical health or safety, and also includes any activity that would subject one to extreme mental stress, such as sleep deprivation, forced

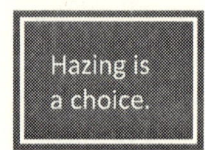

> **Hazing is a choice.**

exclusion from social contact, forced conduct that could result in extreme embarrassment, or other forced activity that could adversely affect the mental health or dignity of the individual. Additionally, the consent of the victim is not a defense to criminal liability. Clearly, Florida has a very broad, strict and specific definition of hazing. Florida has taken a strong stance against an act that most don't even realize is a crime.

There is also a misunderstanding of where hazing occurs and where it originated. Believe it or not, hazing takes place in the military, sports and Ivy League institutions and did not begin at Historically Black Colleges and Universities or within Black Greek Letter Organizations. In fact, hazing origins began in ancient Rome where soldiers were required to overcome feats of pain endurance to become members of the military. Sadly, this is the same basis of hazing today. But why? Well, it seems that hazing is a cycle. When one chooses to haze, a negative cycle of abuse is perpetuated. Consequently, the victim now becomes the abuser.

A victim of hazing has a responsibility to choose to take a stand against the crime or report it. Otherwise, the act remains secret and unfortunately, the cycle will continue.

Jarian N. Lyons is an attorney with Parks and Crump LLC in Tallahassee, Florida. As part of the National Anti-Hazing/Anti-Violence Task Force's initiative to address, "The Culture, Cause and Cure for Hazing," this article first appeared in the Capital Outlook Newspaper on February 24, 2012 entitled, "Hazing is a choice…and a crime."

Cultural Perspective, Linda T. Fortenberry, Ph.D.

I present this summative discourse on hazing from a cultural perspective with a clear bias. Hazing must be eliminated from the culture of our schools and universities and our society in general. In this perspective, I provide a definition of hazing, culture and socialization. I also discuss activities associated with hazing, a blueprint of hazing and five essential steps for changing the culture.

Hazing is defined by the FIPG (Fraternal Information Programming Group) as, "Any action taken or situation created, intentionally, whether on or off fraternity premises, to produce mental or physical discomfort, embarrassment, harassment, or ridicule. Hazing activities may include: use of alcohol; paddling in any form; creation of excessive fatigue; physical and psychological shocks; quests, treasure hunts, scavenger hunts," etc.

According to the Center for Advanced Research on Language Acquisition (2012), culture is defined as the "shared patterns of behaviors and interactions, cognitive constructs, and affective understanding that are learned through a process of socialization. These shared patterns identify the members of a culture group while also distinguishing those of another group." Additionally, socialization is a continuing process whereby an individual acquires a personal identity and learns the norms, values, behavior, and social skills appropriate to his or her social position (Collins English Dictionary, 2012).

When students join groups, they inherit willingly or unwillingly the norms, values and behaviors of their perpetrators. This is supported in both a national study on student hazing at the University of Maine and a publication by Sigma Alpha Epsilon. For instance, an excerpt of these findings note that hazing takes place in a variety of extra-curricular activities and includes behaviors that are pre-meditated, abusive, dangerous, degrading and often illegal and life-threatening.

Because of the respect for their perpetrators, the vast majority of college students do not report hazing to campus officials. They recognize hazing as an integral part of the campus culture.

As such, Lipkins (2006) describes a "blueprint of hazing." She states that "the newcomer or victim, is hazed. Once accepted by the group, the victim becomes a bystander, and watches as others get hazed. Eventually, the bystander achieves senior status and power, and becomes a perpetrator. They do onto others what was done to them, and they feel as though they have the right and duty to pass on the tradition. High school students pack up this blueprint and stuff it into their backpack, in order to take their hazing experience with them to college, the military and the workplace. Each hazing brings with it the possibility of a new twist. Perpetrators want to leave their mark on the tradition, and therefore they may add or change the tradition, slightly."

Furthermore, Lipkins states that "there are also cultural forces in place that do nothing to discourage hazing, and in some cases even promote it as healthy character building." Hazing is ritualistic and based on tradition. Members of the group simply believe it is okay to haze new members because that's the way it has always been done. They feel entitled to make others go through the same things they endured. This attitude toward hazing often carries into adulthood, so at no point in the cycle does anyone see any need for change. Hazing continues year-after-year reinforcing the idea that it promotes positive and healthy group cohesion."

> Members of groups feel it is okay to haze members.

With the countless acts of hazing deaths mentioned in this book, "clearly hazing is not merely a problem of FAMU. Hazing is not merely a problem of club life on college campuses. Hazing is not merely a problem of American higher education. Hazing is a problem of American society, a manifestation of our culture," according to Rogers (2012). It must be eradicated from our culture for a better society. In fact, it can be changed by employing five essential steps according to Nuwer cited in Swigert (2005). They include:

1. Recognizing that hazing is occurring in the educational environment
2. Interpreting the activities of hazing as a problem
3. Getting stakeholders to recognize they have the ability and responsibility to change the culture
4. Educating stakeholders on ways to affect change in the educational environment so they can appropriately confront the problem of hazing
5. Ensuring that stakeholders take action regarding hazing matters

Dr. Linda T. Fortenberry is the national coordinator of the National Save the Family Now Movement, Inc. and director of Education and Development for Bethel Missionary Baptist Church in Tallahassee, Florida. She is also a retired associate superintendent of New Orleans Public Schools.

How To Eradicate Hazing

How to Eradicate Hazing

Step I - Educate Stakeholders

In an old expression, "Ignorance of the law is no excuse." Hazing is "deeply embedded in a dark, demonic and secretive culture" according to Rev. Dr. R.B. Holmes Jr. To participate in hazing ritual is asinine. So, we must eradicate it from the American culture. In fact, we must educate all stakeholders such as students, parents, teachers, administrators and community representatives on the policies, procedures and laws for anti-hazing preventions. Students must know clearly what the policies, procedures and laws are regarding hazing in the educational setting. This information must be very transparent regardless of whether students are participating in extra-curricular activities.

In a national survey at Alfred University, for example, "athletes had little or no knowledge of strategies directly related to hazing prevention on their campuses. Only 15 percent believed that their institutions involved law enforcement in monitoring, investigating, and prosecuting hazing incidents. Only 25 percent of athletes thought the institutions had clear staff expectations in athletics for monitoring and enforcing hazing policy. Only 36 percent of athletes believed that the institutions provided alternative bonding and recognition events

> "Only 15 percent believed that their institutions involved law enforcement in monitoring, investigating and prosecuting hazing incidents."

for teams to prevent hazing. Only 25 percent of athletes thought that their institutions took strong disciplinary and corrective measures for known cases of hazing, yet these were the strategies survey respondents (institutions officials) considered most effective in the prevention of hazing" (Hoover, 1999).

As result, anti-hazing preventions information must be an essential part of the Student Code of Conduct, membership intake, pledge or any extra-curricular activity in the academic setting. Along with the faculty sponsor reviewing the policies, procedures and laws with students on hazing for their respective activity, educational institutions must create anti-hazing training including a campus 24-hour anonymous hazing hotline. Students must complete an assessment questionnaire after the training to prove their knowledge and understanding of hazing, as well as know whom to call if they have any concerns. Educational institutions such as Bowling Green State University use some of these methods through its Online Hazing Education Program.

In addition to completing the assessment questionnaire, students must complete a research paper on hazing. They must also participate in a community service projects regarding anti-hazing preventions before participating or becoming a member of a group. We have to educate our stakeholders on hazing such as students to ensure that they fully understand the seriousness of the matter. With these requirements intact combined with students being officially enrolled in school and maintaining good academic standing, our expectation for student safety and participation in extra-curricular activities will be enhanced and substantiated by interventions as a viable means to eradicate hazing. Figure 4 provides a sample letter for educational institutions to use to educate student stakeholders, support the Student Code of Conduct and provide proof of anti-hazing prevention compliance.

Sample Letter (Figure 4)

John S. Doe University
Office of Student Affairs
5432 Any Street West, Townsville, State 54321

Anti-Hazing Prevention Policy Compliance
(Educate Student Stakeholders)

This letter confirms that I have read, fully understand and completed the following requirements of the John Doe University's Anti-Hazing Prevention Policy.

Specifically, I have completed the Online Hazing Training, assessment questionnaire and know how to report hazing anonymously through the campus 24-hour hotline.

Also, I have completed both a research paper regarding the hazing training and the required community service project regarding anti-hazing prevention.

Hazing Definition

Hazing is "any activity expected of someone to join a group that has the potential to humiliate, degrade, abuse or endanger a person regardless of his or her willingness to participate."

Florida Hazing Law

"Hazing" means any action or situation that recklessly or intentionally endangers the mental or physical health or safety of a student for purposes including, but not limited to, initiation or admission into or affiliation with any organization operating under the sanction of a postsecondary institution. "Hazing" includes, but is not limited to, pressuring or coercing the student into violating state or federal law, any brutality of a physical nature, such as whipping, beating, branding, exposure to the elements, forced consumption of any food, liquor, drug, or other substance, or other forced physical activity that could adversely affect the physical health or safety of the student, and also includes any activity that would subject the student to extreme mental stress, such as sleep deprivation, forced exclusion from social contact, forced conduct that could result in extreme embarrassment, or other forced activity that could adversely affect the mental health or dignity of the student.

An open door to your future. www.johnsdoeuniversity.com

John S. Doe University

Office of Student Affairs
5432 Any Street West, Townsville, State 54321

<u>Anti-Hazing Prevention Policy Compliance</u>
(Educate Student Stakeholders – *cont'd*)

Online Hazing Training

Provides training on the policies, procedures and laws, etc. regarding anti-hazing prevention at John S. Doe University.

Assessment Questionnaire

Provides an assessment of the Online Hazing Training at John S. Doe University for reinforcement of anti-hazing prevention.

Campus 24-hour Hazing Hotline

Affords an opportunity for students to report hazing anonymously at John S. Doe University.

Research Paper

Provides a research paper of student proof of understanding anti-hazing prevention before participating in any extra-curriculum activities at John S. Doe University.

Community Service Project

Provides a community service project of student proof of anti-hazing prevention before participating in any extra-curriculum activities at John S. Doe University.

_____   Office of Student Affairs
Student's Name (Print)

_____   _____
Student's Signature   Dean of Student Affairs' Signature

_____   _____
Date   Date

An open door to your future.   www.johnsdoeuniversity.com

How to Eradicate Hazing

Step II - Review Policies, Procedures and Laws

Having policies, procedures and laws are one thing, but reviewing them are another. To eradicate hazing, we must routinely review the policies, procedures and laws on anti-hazing preventions with all stakeholders such as parents of educational institutions. In Step I of the model, we discussed how to eradicate hazing through the involvement of student stakeholders. In Step II of the model, we provide examples of how to eradicate hazing through the involvement of parent stakeholders.

For example, educational institutions must use social media, newsletters, website, special events and online hazing training to review and discuss periodically the policies, procedures and laws on anti-hazing preventions. Through social media such as Facebook and Twitter, this will give parents an opportunity to periodically review information on hazing and participate in dialogue for improved knowledge and understanding. Also, through newsletters, websites, special events and online hazing training, this will give parents an opportunity to review pertinent information on hazing and participate in anti-hazing prevention programs in the school setting and community. Ultimately, this will provide a paper trail of interventions to eradicate hazing from

> Chapter advisors receive the least amount of training on anti-hazing prevention strategies.

the culture. Figure 5 provides a sample newsletter to parents illustrating John S. Doe University's approach to review the policies and laws of anti-hazing preventions. This same letter could be tailored to chapter advisors, chairpersons and executive officers of campus organizations since they, chapter advisors, receive the least amount of training on anti-hazing prevention strategies (Swigert, 2005).

Sample Newsletter (Figure 5)

John S. Doe University
Office of Student Affairs
5432 Any Street West, Townsville, State 54321

Anti-Hazing Prevention Policy Compliance
(Review Policies and Laws)

Welcome parents to the 2012 – 2013 academic year! This newsletter focuses on the approaches we are using to promote zero tolerance of hazing at John S. Doe University.

These strategies include our social media campaign, monthly newsletter, special events, online hazing training:

SOCIAL MEDIA

We provide parents an opportunity to follow us on Twitter at John S. Doe University to gain the latest information on anti-hazing preventions.

WEBSITE

We have a Hazing Website to display information, review and discuss periodically the policies, procedures and laws on anti-hazing preventions.

ONLINE HAZING TRAINING

We require students to complete an Online Hazing Training at John S. Doe University before they can participate in any extra-curricular activities.

We encourage parents to complete the hazing training to review the policies and laws of anti-hazing preventions.

We enlist parents to help us reinforce the expectation of anti-hazing preventions to all stakeholders at the university.

NEWSLETTER

We will post a monthly newsletter on our website at John S. Doe University to reiterate the policies and laws regarding anti-hazing preventions.

SPECIAL EVENTS

We will promote and participate in special events on the campus of John S. Doe University and the community to review the policies and laws regarding anti-hazing preventions.

Again, we welcome parents to this academic year. Your active involvement is greatly appreciated.

An open door to your future.   www.johnsdoeuniversity.com

How to Eradicate Hazing

Step III - Address Accountability

People drive their automobiles everyday with the understanding of the laws and consequences for breaking the laws. When they break the laws by speeding, reckless driving or driving under the influence of alcohol, they are held accountable. This might include having to attend a driver's education class, suspension or loss of their driver's license. In the same vein, we must address and ensure that all stakeholders such as teachers or educators are held accountable to the policies, procedures and laws on anti-hazing preventions.

In the previous two steps of the model, we noted the need to educate stakeholders and review policies and laws about hazing respectively through the involvement of students and parents. In Step III, we provide examples of how to eradicate hazing through the involvement of teachers and educators. For example, educational institutions must use these stakeholders to address accountability through transparency or evidence such as lesson plans, bulletin boards, newsletters, websites, social media and online hazing training.

In addition to educators and teachers receiving hazing training, school officials must require that teachers make sure the policies, procedures and laws on anti-hazing preventions are a part of their course syllabi. For accountability, school officials, particularly K – 12, can assess evidence of this being communicated accordingly through visiting and communicating with teachers in their classrooms, reviewing department chairs' accountability folders and/or posting of syllabi on institutions' websites. Just as drivers of automobiles are held accountable for driving safely, teachers must be held accountable for communicating information so the message about anti-hazing prevention is reinforced and taken seriously throughout the educational environment. Figure 6 provides a sample of an abbreviated teacher science prep course syllabus to show or address accountability of hazing through transparency. As mentioned in a previous chapter, Nuwer cited in Swigert (2005) discusses five steps to eradicate hazing from the culture. This example mirrors one of the steps since the goal is to give teachers the skills to employ measurable interventions designed to affect change in a society or particularly the culture of hazing in the educational environment.

Furthermore, school boards must hold educators such as administrators accountable for ensuring that they are taking proactive means to address accountability regarding anti-hazing preventions, as well as investigating fully incidents of hazing allegations at the highest level possible. Courts are bombarded with legal cases and decisions to determine if institutions have a "duty of care" or duty to protect" hazing victims. In a hazing incident (1993) at the University of Nebraska, for example, the Nebraska Supreme Court ruled that the university had a duty to protect a fraternity pledge who was severely injured (brain-damaged) while trying to escape fraternity members who were hazing him on the university property (Reisberg, 1999).

> Send a clear anti-hazing message to stakeholders by establishing a record of taking action against suspected and known cases of hazing.

To address accountability, Hoover (1999) recommends administrators (1) send a clear anti-hazing message to stakeholders by establishing a record of taking action against suspected and known cases of hazing; (2) expect responsibility, integrity and civility by requiring staff to screen potential students for behavioral and academic problems and (3) require organized initiation events according to school policies. Additionally, Hughes (2008) provides 10 steps administrators can take to address accountability regarding various forms of violence on their campuses. Please see figure 7 which mirrors another step or strategy of Nuwer to change the culture of hazing by taking action.

Sample Course Syllabus (Figure 6)

John S. Doe University
Office of Student Affairs
5432 Any Street West, Townsville, State 54321

Teacher Science Prep Course Syllabus
Spring 2013

Anti-Hazing Prevention Policy Compliance
(Address Accountability)

Course Description

The purpose of this course is to provide test-taking strategies to prepare students for the science portion of the exit exam.

Course Topics

Physical Science, Biology and Process/Research Skills

School Rules & Expectation

Understand that hazing is dangerous because it is: "any activity expected of someone to join a group that has the potential to humiliate, degrade, abuse or endanger a person regardless of his or her willingness to participate"

Understand that hazing is illegal as stated by Florida Hazing Law:

1) As used in this section, "hazing" means any action or situation that recklessly or intentionally endangers the mental or physical health or safety of a student for purposes including, but not limited to, initiation or admission into or affiliation with any organization operating under the sanction of a postsecondary institution. "Hazing" includes, but is not limited to, pressuring or coercing the student into violating state or federal law, any brutality of a physical nature, such as whipping, beating, branding, exposure to the elements, forced consumption of any food, liquor, drug, or other substance, or other forced physical activity that could adversely affect the physical health or safety of the student, and also includes any activity that would subject the student to extreme mental stress, such as sleep deprivation, forced exclusion from social contact, forced conduct that could result in extreme embarrassment, or other forced activity that could adversely affect the mental health or dignity of the student.

I have read, fully understand and agree to John Doe University's anti-hazing prevention policy:

_____   _____
Student's Name (Print)   Student's Signature

                                                             _____
                                                             Date

An open door to your future.   www.johnsdoeuniversity.com

10 Steps for Administrators to Report Violence (Figure 7)

Anti-Hazing Prevention Policy Compliance
(Address Accountability)

1. Document the Incident

    Document the details of the incident according to the reporting party, including who made the threat, what occurred, who else was involved, and when and where the event took place. This information should be recorded on the Incident Report Form.

2. Notify the Reporting Party

    Notify the reporting party that the school is investigating the incident and that a member of the Campus Violence Prevention Team will notify the reporting party as to the outcome of the investigation. In the interest of protecting confidentiality and privacy, some details surrounding the incident should not be revealed to the reporting party.

3. Visit the Incident Site

    Visit the incident site and obtain a detailed description. Document the characteristics of the site on the Incident Report Form.

4. Interview All Witnesses

    Interview the witnesses privately to obtain accounts of the event. Witness statements should be documented on the Incident Report Form.

5. Interview the Alleged Perpetrator

    Interview the alleged perpetrator separately to obtain his or her description of the incident. The description should be recorded on the Incident Report Form. The alleged perpetrator should be informed of the Campus Violence Prevention Policy, and of the school's practice of investigating all reports of violent threats or behaviors.

6. Escort Alleged Perpetrator off Campus if necessary

    Escort the alleged perpetrator off campus property, if appropriate. In instances when the threat or act of violence is serious, or there is potential for the alleged perpetrator's behavior to escalate, he or she should be suspended and escorted off campus grounds by security. Depending on the nature of the threat, security may need to be armed. The perpetrator should be informed that an investigation will ensue, and that he or she may be contacted to participate in the investigation. The Team should also notify the alleged perpetrator if he or she is prohibited from returning to campus.

Anti-Hazing Prevention Policy Compliance
(Address Accountability – cont'd)

7. Notify Law Enforcement if necessary

   Notify local law enforcement immediately following an incident. In cases where the potential for violence or injury is not as serious, the Team Leader, head of security, and legal should decide whether law enforcement must be notified.

8. Contact Appropriate Team Members

   Contact additional Team Members to participate in the investigation. The circumstances of the incident will determine which Team members need to be involved. For example, legal should participate when issues regarding the law are involved in the incident, and security personnel should participate if there is potential for serious harm. In the case of an employee or faculty perpetrator, the human resource director should be contacted.

9. Select Mental Health Referral Option

   Select one of the following referral options. When the Team is uncertain about which option is most appropriate, the matter should be discussed with other Team members such as the legal and mental health representatives. Referral options include: (1) Campus Counseling, recommended when an assessment is made of low intent to harm, and when the perpetrator displays insight or remorse. This option is only appropriate for student-perpetrators. (2) Employee Assistance Program, recommended for employee or faculty perpetrators. (3) Outside Mental Health Referral, recommended when the perpetrator displays bizarre or unusual thoughts or behavior. This option is appropriate for employee or faculty perpetrators.

10. Select Suspension Option

    Determine options for modified education or employment, suspension, expulsion or prosecution. The appropriate option should be chosen based on all available information, and the nature of the incident: (1) the perpetrator continues attending school or work; (2) the perpetrator's school/work situation is modified; (3) the perpetrator is given a verbal or written warning; the perpetrator is suspended for an allotted amount of time; (4) the perpetrator is expelled/terminated and (4) the perpetrator is prosecuted.

How to Eradicate Hazing

Step IV - Distinguish Hazing Myths & Truths

While hazing is about power, control, reciprocity and secrecy, students do not understand the seriousness and dangers of hazing. They have misconceptions about hazing which contributes to a continuation of harmful psychological and physical acts of hazing violence in our educational institutions.

In a 2007 publication on hazing prevention in college athletics and a 1988 publication by Sigma Alpha Epsilon, the NCAA and StopHazing.org respectively discussed hazing myths and facts. In view of those publications and other expert opinions from constituents in higher education, the following are some common myths and facts about hazing:

Myth: All initiation rites are acceptable standards and are not harmful to students.

Fact: Students encounter the risk of being hurt physically and emotionally when participating in unacceptable initiation rites. Educational institutions must teach students acceptable initiation rites such as community service projects and mentoring programs.

Myth: Hazing builds a strong legacy and provides continuity and stability of the organization.

Fact: Hazing endangers a person's livelihood. Organizations must build their legacy on scholarship, service and respect for all humankind.

Myth: Hazing is simply about students expressing themselves freely with others.

Fact: When hazed, students lose their own thoughts, are punished and disallowed to communicate with others outside of the organization. They are victimized and powerless.

Myth: Hazing is new to our society.

Fact: Hazing is not new to our society. It was first documented by Greek philosopher Plato in 387 B.C. and in the U.S. at Harvard College in 1657.

Myth: Hazing happens only at the college and university levels.

Fact: Hazing occurs in various facets of our American culture including the elementary, middle and high school levels; military, sports and the workplace. It also crosses racial, ethnic, gender and class boundaries.

Myth: Hazing is not a crime when students agree to participate in unacceptable initiation rites.

Fact: Hazing is illegal in 44 states. Just because students agree to participate is not a defense against criminal liability. Hazing is a crime.

How to Eradicate Hazing

Myth: Educational institutions have done all they can do to combat hazing.

Fact: Hazing is rooted or ingrained in the social structure of educational institutions. Through a "code of silence," hazing protects a socialized process. The "code of silence" maintains and legitimizes hazing as a normal and acceptable act within the organization.

Myth: Members of groups feel it is okay to haze other members because of tradition.

Fact: It is never appropriate to haze. Hazing demonstrates a lack of compassion for others and themselves.

> No level of hazing is appropriate.

Myth: Hazing is not a choice.

Fact: Hazing is a choice. It takes two or more individuals to participate in unacceptable initiation rites.

Myth: Hazing is an integral part of the education institutions' culture so it can't be changed.

Fact: Change is inevitable. As a society, we must publicly denounce hazing and implement anti-hazing prevention strategies across the nation.

Myth: The determination of hazing activities is ambiguous.

Fact: Any activity where an individual is being physically and psychologically abused, deprived of sleep, consuming alcohol, participating in sexual acts and paddling are clear examples of hazing activities. If perpetrators and victims would have a difficult time of telling their loved ones and school officials that these activities were a part of their organization's rituals, then it is clearly an unacceptable act.

                        ∽

Myth: Hazing is fun and harmless.

Fact: Hazing is detrimental to our children, but they are eager to belong to an organization and willingly or unwillingly to be abused by members of the organization. Educational institutions must provide anti-hazing prevention strategies and processes for our children to recognize and report hazing incidents.

                        ∽

Myth: Hazing improves socialization in an organization.

Fact: Hazing promotes social oppression in an organization that forms power and control over those who are victimized or perceived as less powerful in the organization.

Educational institutions should discuss the myths and truths of hazing with all constituents (students, parents, teachers, etc.) through seminars and conferences, as well as make the information a part of their online training. Educational institutions such as Bowling State University have an Online Hazing Education Program that explains the myths and truths of hazing for improved learning.

How to Eradicate Hazing

Step V - Implement Activities

It is written that "we learn best by doing." To eradicate hazing from our American culture, we must implement activities that bring attention to the hazing. In the first three steps of the model, we noted the need to educate stakeholders, review policies and laws and address accountability about hazing respectively through the involvement of students, parents and educators. In the fourth step of the model, we distinguished the myths and truths of hazing. In Step V, we provide examples of how to eradicate hazing through the involvement of community organizations. One such community organization that is pressing to eradicate hazing from our culture is the National Anti-Hazing/Anti-Violence Task Force.

The NAHAVT was announced during a press conference at the National Press Club in Washington, D.C. on January 17, 2012, where a consortium of leading organizational representatives such as Rev. Dr. R.B. Holmes Jr., founder and chairman of the NAHAVT, Dr. George Cooper president of South Carolina State and attorney Lezli Baskerville president and chief officer of the National Association for Equal Opportunity in Higher Education vowed they would not cease until hazing is eradicated. This historic conference was birthed from the tragic death

> NAHAVT launched at the National Press Club to eradicate hazing from our culture.

of drum major Robert Champion of Florida A&M University. Under the leadership of Rev. Dr. R.B. Holmes Jr., NAHAVT proposed and implemented the following activities of its 12-point three- year plan (2012 – 2015) to eradicate hazing. Figure 8 provides a diagram of the 12 Point Plan.

1. Convened the first annual Hazing Conference on February 24-25, 2012 at South Carolina State University in Orangeburg, South Carolina.
2. Conducted Hazing Awareness on March 25, 2012 with a coalition of religious leaders and denominational leaders who will develop and execute the plan of action. Prayer ministries across America will make the "12 Point Plan" an active agenda item and regularly lift it to God in prayer.
3. Sponsor annually Engagement and Empowerment Rallies that include a series of community forums sponsored by city mayors, community organizations, student government organizations and the Martin Luther King Center for Non-Violent Social Change. These "Engagement and Empowerment Rallies" will be held in twenty-five cities over the next three years (2012-2015).
4. Conduct a Youth Summit in Atlanta, Georgia and other cities in conjunction with the National Newspaper Publishers Association.
5. Design an Anti-Hazing Curriculum that is targeted to public and private schools to teach young people transformational solutions to resist hazing and bullying. This initiative will begin in 2012 in Title I schools in urban and rural communities.
6. Foster a Black Press Initiative designed to utilize African-American newspapers to carry monthly articles on "The Culture, Cause and Cure for Hazing." African-American broadcasters will be encouraged to develop "talk shows" focused on the eradication.
7. Implement a Social Media Initiative designed to utilize all of the appropriate social media (i.e. internet, Facebook, Twitter, YouTube, blogs, etc.) to inform the community of the efforts to eradicate hazing from our culture and community.
8. Initiate a Media Campaign with groups such as BET, WORD

How to Eradicate Hazing

Network, C-Span, TV One, and other media venues to develop a comprehensive plan of action to blitz their respective listening audiences to foster a movement to address and eliminate "hazing" from our culture.

9. Collaborate with Historically Black Colleges and Universities (HBCU), HBCU presidents, administrators and student leaders to consistently spearhead workshops and conferences to eliminate hazing on and off campuses, while concurrently, strengthening policies and programs that clearly state that hazing is unacceptable.
10. Collaborate with pastors and theologians in developing sermons and lectures on the dangers of hazing and strategies for its elimination, as well as encourage psychologists and sociologists to develop position papers on the subject *(See sample sermon in figure 9).*
11. Implement a Recognition Program to recognize persons, groups, organizations, universities, colleges, businesses, media venue and others who have developed exemplary programs to eradicate hazing from our culture and community.
12. Promote the Robert Champion Scholarship Initiative designed to work with the Robert Champion Foundation, Inc. and encourage HBCUs to establish a Robert Champion Scholarship on campuses to forever spotlight the importance of the elimination of hazing on all campuses in general and HBCUs in particular.

As we consistently implement these activities coupled with others throughout the nation, this will serve a strong means to eradicate hazing from our K-12 schools and colleges.

Figure 8.

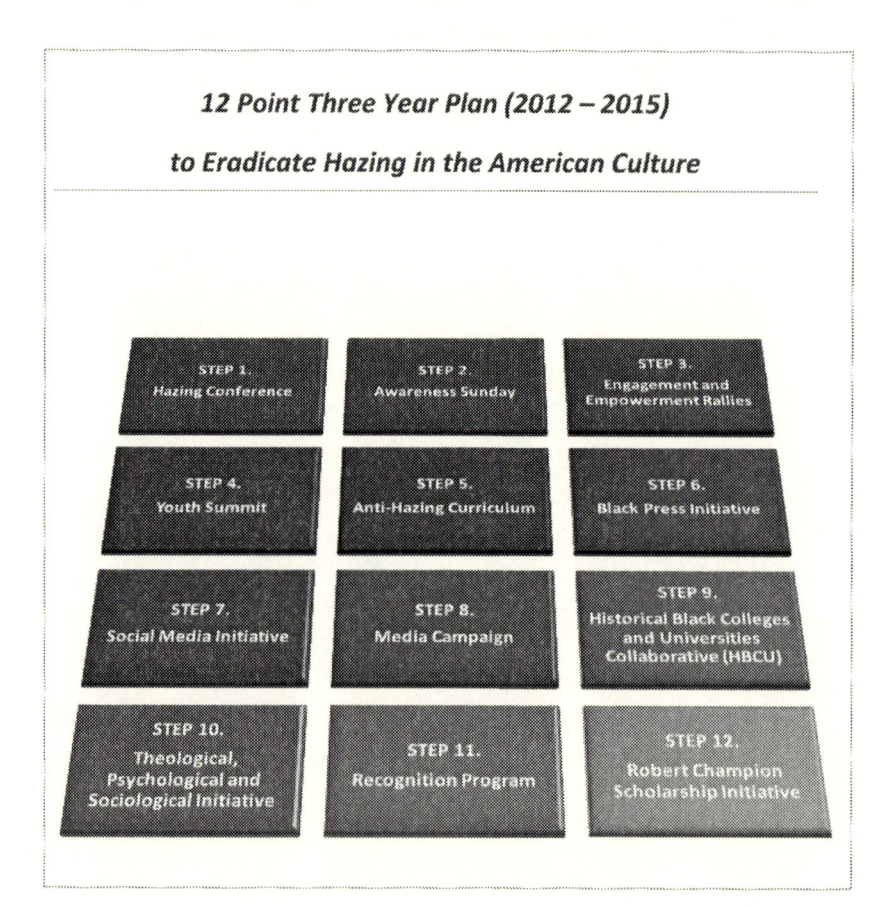

12 Point Three Year Plan (2012 – 2015)
to Eradicate Hazing in the American Culture

STEP 1. Hazing Conference	STEP 2. Awareness Sunday	STEP 3. Engagement and Empowerment Rallies
STEP 4. Youth Summit	STEP 5. Anti-Hazing Curriculum	STEP 6. Black Press Initiative
STEP 7. Social Media Initiative	STEP 8. Media Campaign	STEP 9. Historical Black Colleges and Universities Collaborative (HBCU)
STEP 10. Theological, Psychological and Sociological Initiative	STEP 11. Recognition Program	STEP 12. Robert Champion Scholarship Initiative

Figure 9

Excerpt of Rev. Dr. R.B. Holmes Jr.'s Sermon

What is the answer to the eradication of hazing?
By Ronald W. Holmes, Ph.D.

"I have been a victim of a selfish kind of love. I am starting with the man in the mirror" are the lyrics to Michael Jackson's song, "Man in the Middle." It reflects that a change of behavior and attitude in making the world a better place to live, work and grow starts within each individual. Many individuals and groups have tried different methods to change the culture of hazing at our educational institutions. Consequently, laws have been passed in 44 states to end hazing but it continues to occur in various institutions nationwide.

So the critical questions to be asked are: What is the answer to the eradication of hazing? What scripture provides meaning to the eradication of hazing? What are three essential points Reverend Dr. R.B. Holmes Jr. provides for eliminating hazing from our culture?

Because of the tragic death of former Florida A&M University's drum major Robert Champion, Reverend Dr. R.B. Holmes Jr., pastor of Bethel Missionary Baptist Church in Tallahassee, Florida launched the National Anti-Hazing/Anti-Violence Task Force at the National Press Club in Washington D.C. on January 17, 2012. The task force's primary goal is to eradicate violence and hazing from the culture of educational institutions. As part of the task force initiative, Holmes spoke recently to his congregation at the first annual Anti-Hazing/Anti-Violence Awareness Sunday on the subject, "Godly guidelines for victorious living" with a focus on eradicating hazing from our school culture. This message was supported by the biblical text from the Book of James, Chapter 1: verses 19 – 27.

According to Holmes, the bible says in verse 25 "but whoever looketh into the perfect law of liberty; and continueth in it; he being not a forgetful hearer but doer of the work; this man shall be blessed in his deed." In essence, Holmes explains that "when we abide in God's word, strive to live according to His word, His ordinances and His standards, we will be blessed. The reason is that God has the answer for all of our questions, God knows how to resolve all of our problems, God can supply all of our needs and God can heal all of our hurts and diseases."

Unfortunately, we get in trouble because we don't listen to God, Holmes claims. In fact, we spend days and years in the wilderness engaging in immoral, illegal and irresponsible acts such as hazing because we ignore the blessings that are in the word. So, "the answer to the eradication of hazing, inequality, sin and depression in our schools, community and workplace is in the word. The word can fix our frustration, mend our broken hearts, revive our wounded soul. God has given the guideline, His word, for victorious living," according to Holmes.

Holmes further emphasizes in his message that for the students and other people to live victoriously in accordance with the Book of James, "we must be (1) open to God's word; (2) obedient to God's word and (3) motivated by God's word." Being open to God's word (James 1: 19 -22), Holmes says "we have to demonstrate that we have a capacity to listen, a controlled tongue, a calm spirit and a clean life. Allowing people to haze us such as drinking and being beaten is not being open to the word." As an alternative, we must tell our perpetrators that we are not tolerating hazing because we have God's word. We will participate only in acceptable initiation activities.

Second, Holmes says we must be obedient to God's word (James 1: 22 – 25). While recent allegations of hazing has surfaced at Florida A&M University such as the Alpha Kappa Psi Fraternity and a female dance team, Holmes says that "Interim President Larry Robinson has told students there is a zero tolerance for hazing because hazing is wrong. Now, it is time for our students to start doing according to the word." They must look in the mirror and make a change by stop being the perpetrators or victims of hazing. They know what hazing has done to our universities, so they must not be disobedient to God and go back and be a part of hazing. They must remember that hazing is immoral and deadly.

Third, Holmes says that we must be motivated by God's word (James 1: 26 -27), which require us to "guard our tongue, life and give to others." Students must keep themselves unspotted from the world by disallowing people to haze them in order to be a part of a group. Being a Christian does not constitute individuals being hurt socially, psychologically and physically. Christians must not use their religion in vain. In lieu of hazing, students must learn appropriate initiation rites such as community service projects and mentoring programs. There are a lot of people in need that can benefit from their community spirit of giving.

As part of the hazing task force, Holmes is encouraging other theologians of churches nationwide to have Anti-hazing/Anti-Violence Worship Services to develop sermons and lectures on the dangers of hazing and methods for its eradication. While students may willingly or unwillingly participate in hazing, Holmes' message is very clear: Students should remove themselves from being "a victim of a selfish kind of love." Hazing is demeaning, dangerous and deadly. The answer to the eradication of hazing is in God's word.

How to Eradicate Hazing

Step VI - Communicate Impact

The old Negro spiritual reminds us that, "We shall overcome someday" despite the pain, suffering, trials and tribulations confronting our lives. Hazing impacts the victims as well as their families. To eradicate hazing, we must understand the impact and communicate this impact has on the lives of citizens.

In Steps 1 – 5 of the model, we noted the need to educate stakeholders, review policies, procedures and laws, address accountability, distinguish the hazing myths and truths and implement activities to prevent hazing through the involvement of students, parents, educators and community organizations. Giving respect to all victims of hazing (1838 – 2012), we communicate in this step of the model the tragic impact of hazing through the death of Robert D. Champion Jr. We discuss his background and how the Robert D. Champion family hopes to bring attention to the impact of hazing through the Robert Champion Foundation, Inc.

Following is the interview conducted with Robert Champion's mother and father, Mr. and Mrs. Robert and Pamela Champion.

Background of Robert D. Champion Jr.

Pamela Champion recalls Robert as a good person and clearly a people person. He had a passion and like for people. He referred to everyone as, "his friend." He was a Christian who believed in God and was baptized at the age of nine. He was a good boy with a great personality.

He was someone who Mrs. Champion saw as not having any enemies. She had never seen Robert get mad at anyone including his two sisters. He would always say to Mrs. Champion, "It's not that serious." Robert volunteered playing the drums in church at age 14, as well as taught himself how to play the keyboard at church. He was a very determined person, committed to following through on a given task, once he "got it his head." Robert's favorite church song was "99 ½ Won't Do," because he strived for perfection.

Robert Champion, Sr. was very proud of his son and proud to be his father. According to Robert Senior, Robert was a good son and knew what he wanted to be in life. Mr. Champion wanted him to be a football player but Robert had other thoughts. His interest, in fact, was music. Robert was blessed to play and teach music. He was the type of person who helped other people. Mr. Champion never heard of his son being in fights or getting into any trouble. He never had to get him out of jail. To see him go from washing pots in the kitchen to being a drum major in one of the biggest bands in the nation was amazing to Mr. Champion. Robert did what he enjoyed doing - playing in the marching band at FAMU. He was determined to play in the band even when his band uniform was too small. Robert Jr. worked extremely hard one summer to lose the necessary weight so he could fit into his uniform.

At the age of five years old, Robert was first introduced to a marching band when Mrs. Champion took him to a parade. From that moment, he started practicing to become a drum major. He would march with a broomstick or rake up and down the driveway to practice being a drum major. For Christmas, Mrs. Champion, recalls, Robert wanted a drum major cape instead of toys. In the fifth grade, Robert started playing the clarinet, and coordinated his first talent show performance by himself. While his siblings made fun of

> Robert Champion was known as "90 degrees" at SWD because of the way he raised his legs while marching.

him, he continued to practice for the talent show. Mrs. Champion was so proud of Robert and his performance. The talent performance showed his demeanor, commitment, determination and passion for music.

In junior high school, Robert's music teacher recognized his abilities. He was very excited about being a part of the marching band at Southwest DeKalb High (SWD) School. During the eight grade, he was always the last one out of the band room making sure everything was okay. SWD band director said he was the perfect band student because he would practice and then know the materials the next day. In fact, he was known as "90 degrees" at SWD because of the way he raised his legs while marching.

By the end of 10th grade, Robert became a drum major at SWD. In his junior year, he performed in the movie, *Drumline*. Robert was also instrumental behind the scene in *Drumline*. The producers would film him so the actors could learn his steps. His motto was, "Choose to do your best, then out do yourself." The Champions never had a problem spotting Robert on the field because he could jump higher than other band members. When the band played "Saving the best for last," Robert would always be the last one to run and jump through a band routine because of his exemplary performance. He gave more than 100 percent.

> Robert Champion was known as "The Example" while in FAMU's marching band.

While in FAMU's marching band, Robert was known as "The Example." These words were engraved inside his marching band hat. Robert loved to choreograph performances and enjoyed volunteering his talents at Clark Atlanta University's band camp during the summer. He also enjoyed lifting a person's spirit. Mrs. Champion recalls Robert performing for a lady at FAMU whose son loved to see Robert perform. Robert would march up and down the person's driveway for the child to see him perform at close range. After graduating from FAMU, Robert's goal was to become a teacher at SWD, as well produce music.

Impact of Hazing, Mr. & Mrs. Robert Champion

Robert D. Champion Jr. was born on July 13, 1985 and died on November 19, 2011. The cause of the death was homicide due to a hazing ritual where he was kicked and beaten with drum sticks and bass-drum mallets according to evidence released by prosecutors from the Orange-Osceola State Attorney's Office. The medical examiner for

Orange County reported specifically that Robert died of "hemorrhagic shock due to soft tissue hemorrhage involving multiple blunt trauma blows to his body" (Winter, 2011). Florida prosecutors charged 13 people in connection with the hazing death of Robert Champion where 11 faced felony charges and two faced misdemeanor hazing charges.

According to Mrs. Champion, dealing with the loss of her son is a minute-to-minute matter. Robert was one year old when she and her family moved into their house. She says that any opening of the doors in the house can take her to a down moment. Her toughest days or hardest times are usually between 11:00 p.m. – 12:00 p.m. because this was the time she would call Robert or he would call her from FAMU. When she thinks of him, she cannot get the thoughts out of her head of what he was going through at FAMU. Mrs. Champion says there is not a day she doesn't face depression.

Similarly, Mr. Champion says that it is very hard dealing with the loss of Robert because he was his only son. For Robert Jr. to have accomplished what he did in life, Mr. Champion says it makes him focus on making sure this does not happen to another child. Mr. Champion says he knew his son was not the type of person who would hurt anyone. His objective now is to make sure his son's life was not in vain because he believes the work his son started is not finished.

As result of the death of her son, Mrs. Champion says the whole focus now is to carry out the mission of the Robert Champion Foundation, Inc. According to the Champions, "We want to create educational programs at the elementary, middle and high school levels to bring about awareness of hazing. We want to teach real-life examples of what hazing is doing and fully educate K – 12 students about the causes and effects of hazing. We want to end hazing."

Further, Mr. Champion added that they have established a hazing hotline (1-855-N-Hazing or 1-855-642-9464). Students can call the hotline anonymously if they are being hazed or bullied or know of someone who is being hazed or bullied. Figure 10, provides a description of the history, vision, mission, goals, objectives and programs of the Robert Champion Foundation, Inc. The website address is: **www.drummajorforchange.com/HOME/**

Figure 10.

Robert Champion Drum Major for Change Foundation, Inc.

History:

The Robert D. Champion Drum Major for Change Foundation, Inc. came into existence on December 27, 2011. Inspired by the untimely and targeted death of Robert Darnell Champion, a Florida Agricultural and Mechanical University (FAMU) Marching 100 drum major. Robert D. Champion was a true leader and an advocate against hazing and violence of any kind. Tragically, he lost his life on November 19, 2011 at the hands of his fellow band members and band alumni in an alleged hazing incident. It was because of this barbaric act against another human being in the divine name of hazing, that the Robert D. Champion Drum Major for Change Foundation mission is to eradicate hazing and its deeply rooted culture of secrecy that has infected the campus of our schools and universities. It is time to take a stand and say, "NO MORE."

Vision:

To eradicate hazing nationwide!

Mission:

To create awareness of the culture of hazing and eliminate the mentality that has influenced countless individuals into the hazing lifestyle.

Robert Champion Drum Major for Change Foundation, Inc.

Goals and Objectives:

- Educate the community on the effects of hazing
- Prevent further casualties caused by the practice of hazing
- Provide empowerment initiatives geared towards public awareness
- Present potential solutions to stamp out the custom of hazing
- Define and identify the meaning of hazing

Programs:

C.H.A.M.P. (Creating Hazing Awareness with Mentality Progression)
A program put together by a team of college students to create awareness of the mental, physical, and emotional effects of hazing within our Historically Black Colleges and Universities, Predominately White Colleges and Universities, and other various organizations; while providing initiatives to ultimately offer solutions to end the inhuman acts of hazing.

Program Slogan: #IAmChampion – We are all "Champions" whether we realize it or not. "We are all exposed to the culture of hazing directly or indirectly in our everyday lives."

How to Eradicate Hazing

Step VII - Advertise using Media

The London 2012 Olympics drew a record television audience of 27.3 million people watching the opening ceremony. Using the television networks and other media (radio stations, newspapers, Twitter, Facebook, etc.) as the framework, we must advertise continuously researched-based solutions and best practices from various educational and community organizations such as the National Anti-Hazing/Anti-Violence Task Force to eradicate hazing from the American society.

As mentioned in Step V, NAHAVT proposed a 12 Point Plan with three components involving the media. They include a:

1. Media Campaign designed to work with groups such as BET, WORD Network, C-Span, TV One, and other media venues to develop a comprehensive plan of action to blitz their respective listening audiences to foster a movement to address and eliminate "hazing" from our culture.
2. Black Press Initiative designed to utilize African-American newspapers to carry monthly articles on the culture, cause and cure for hazing. African American broadcasters will be encouraged to develop "talk shows" focused on the eradication of hazing from American culture.
3. Social Media Initiative designed to utilize all of the appropriate social media (i.e. internet, Facebook, Twitter, YouTube, blogs,

etc.) to inform the community of the effort to eradicate hazing from our culture and community.

It is time to eradicate hazing from the American culture with an emphasis on commercializing researched-based solutions and best practices and publicly denouncing hazing as a major societal issue through the media. The former will allow our educational institutions nationwide to review and adopt these practices in their institutions and communities, as well as talk about the successes for others to follow. The latter will send a strong message to the US population that hazing is unacceptable, unimportant and unnecessary for belonging to a group. In September 2012, for example, more than 100 students affiliated with Greek organizations at Binghamton University gathered at the campus' library to publicly denounce hazing. Students expressed resentment of being stereotyped and associated with hazing (Galloway, 2012). This type of stance against hazing has to happen throughout the country and reported in the media consistently. For information on additional organizations advocating for the eradication of hazing, please see the resource section of this book.

> It is time to eradicate hazing from the American culture with an emphasis on commercializing researched-based solutions through the media.

How to Eradicate Hazing

Step VIII - Teach Anti-Hazing Curriculum

Hazing is an integral part of the American culture. In addition to the educational environment, hazing is in the military, workplace and movie industry. While in the military and workplace respectively, hazing is affiliated with duress, physical trials and public derogation, as well as unreasonable deadlines, excessive workloads and intimidation according to Chang (2011). As a component of the workplace, hazing is a continuing tradition in the National Football League (NFL) and other professional sports without any sanctions. In the NFL, for example, rookies are hazed by veteran players as part of the initiation and acceptance into the league. Some examples of hazing rookies include cutting their hair in peculiar ways and having them to carry veterans' football workout gear. In some teams, rookies are taped to the goal posts while sprayed with mustard, ketchup, mayonnaise or whipped cream.

Because of the potential psychological and physical harm to the athletes and the refusal of players such as Dallas Cowboys Dez Bryant to carry Roy Jones' workout gear, two NFL coaches in 2011 banned the traditional hazing ritual. Dallas Cowboys' coach Jason Garrett and Jacksonville Jaguars' former coach Jack Del Rio opposed the ritual. Del Rio apparently felt compelled to protect his first-round draft choice and rookie quarterback Blaine Gabbert from any undue stress or harm especially since he was drafted to compete for the starting quarterback position against veteran quarterback David Garrard.

Regarding the movie industry, hazing is glamorized in movies such as Carrie. In the 1976 movie Carrie, a young girl who does not make friends easily is humiliated, harassed and abused by her classmates particularly when she becomes the homecoming queen. In fact, while at the prom, the queen and king ballots are rigged so that Carrie and Tommy can win the crown. Just as it appears Carrie is finally accepted among her senior classmates, she is drenched with a bucket of pig's blood with the majority of the student body and others laughing at her.

So to eradicate hazing from the American culture, we must help students get rid of those practices or unacceptable initiation rites they have learned or made a part of their organizations and lifestyles. Some of these devious acts may include abusing and beating individuals and destroying private property. Just as we teach English across the curriculum, we must teach anti-hazing prevention strategies across the curriculum that are researched-oriented for students in the K – 12 setting, particularly, and higher education. In fact, this model must reflect a multi-disciplined approach that provides year-long training and activities to all parties (students, parents, teachers, administrators and community partners) about the dangers of hazing. For students, overall, the training must teach acceptable initiation rites such as community service projects and mentoring programs. For student athletics, particularly, the following is recommended by Hoover cited in Swigert (2005):

> Train coaches and athletes on the importance of initiation rites and the ways to conduct them.

1. Write a policy on the philosophy and goals of initiation rites in athletics
2. Train coaches and athletes on the importance of initiation rites and the ways to conduct them
3. Integrate initiation philosophy and goals into team goal-setting and problem solving
4. Develop community events for the entire athletic department

5. Require organized initiation events for each team prior to each season
6. Recognize athletes as leaders in academic, personal, business and community arenas
7. Rely on the Student Athletic Advisory Committee to promote acceptable initiation rites

For teachers, the training must teach ways to incorporate activities in the lesson such as essays on hazing preventions. For community partners, the training must promote anti-hazing activities in the media. For school administrators, the training must help them to evaluate the effectiveness of the activities on hazing preventions and provide monthly reports to the school board. In a national survey at Alfred University, for example, only 25 percent of athletes thought the institutions had clear expectations in athletics for monitoring and enforcing hazing policy.

How to Eradicate Hazing

Step IX - Evaluate Strategies

Hazing is similar to a cancer. In order to end it, you have to determine the cause for the problem, provide the appropriate interventions or strategies and then monitor the effectiveness of the strategies to determine if the problem is resolved. In the first eight steps of the model, we discussed the plan for eradicating hazing from the American culture. Step IX of the model is to evaluate periodically the anti-hazing prevention strategies at educational institutions.

As mentioned in the book, students "athletes had little or no knowledge of strategies directly related to hazing prevention on their campuses. Only 15 percent believed that their institutions involved law enforcement in monitoring, investigating, and prosecuting hazing incidents. Only 25 percent of athletes thought the institutions had clear staff expectations in athletics for monitoring and enforcing hazing policy. Only 25 percent of athletes thought that their institutions took strong disciplinary and corrective measures for known cases of hazing, yet these were the strategies survey respondents (institutions officials) considered most effective in the prevention of hazing" (Hoover, 1999).

> "Only 25 percent of athletes thought that their institutions took strong disciplinary and corrective measures for known cases of hazing."

As such, we propose concepts of the Malcolm Baldrige Model (See, Plan, Do, Check). While using this model in a previous educational setting, it required us to (1) "See" or assess what the needs were in the educational environment; (2)"Plan" appropriately the goals in line with the needs or assessment of the environment; (3) "Do" or carryout the necessary activities to meet the goals and (4) "Check" or evaluate activities to determine if the goals were met. Figure 11 provides an illustration of this model to evaluate the nine strategies mentioned in this book to eradicate hazing from the American culture of our educational institutions and community. For effectiveness, educational institutions must establish an anti-hazing committee to work closely with the appropriate school officials at the secondary and postsecondary levels. Because hazing is deeply rooted in the American culture, educational institutions must hire the necessary support staff such as a hazing compliance director or administrator who report directly to the top institutions' officials.

(Figure 11)

Evaluate Strategies of Model

See — Assess the educational environment and understand the meaning of hazing from a historical, psychological, sociological, theological, legal and cultural perspective.

Plan — Educate stakeholders; review policies, procedures and laws; address accountability; implement activities; communicate impact; advertise using media; teach anti-hazing curriculum.

Do — Incorporate the Nine Steps of the model, particularly, NAHAVT's 12 Point Plan and other researched-based anti-hazing prevention activities.

Check — Evaluate periodically the Nine Steps of the model, particularly, NAHAVT's 12 Point Plan and other researched-based anti-hazing prevention activities.

Resources

The Holmes Education Post, an education focused Internet newspaper that provides information on improving education. The website address is: theholmeseducationpost.com. What can you find on this site?

- Educational articles to support students, parents, teachers, school administrators, professors and college administrators
- Ideas and educational best practices
- Listing of high school, undergraduate and graduate scholarships
- Videotapes of classroom lectures that demonstrates teaching methods such as Whole Brain Instruction
- Recordings of talk shows on various educational topics
- Books that focus on improving education

The Robert D Champion Drum Major for Change Foundation, Inc.

http://www.drummajorforchange.com/HOME/

Mission: To create awareness of the culture of hazing and eliminate the mentality that has influenced countless individuals into the hazing lifestyle.

The Gordie Foundation - http://www.gordie.org/

The Gordie Foundation was created in 2004 after Gordie Bailey, a freshman at The University of Colorado, died of an alcohol overdose as a result of fraternity hazing. Founded by Gordie's family, the Foundation is dedicated to providing today's young people with the skills to navigate the dangers of alcohol, binge drinking, peer pressure, and hazing.

The Gordie Center for Substance Abuse Prevention

The Gordie Center for Substance Abuse Prevention was created in 2010 through a merger between The Gordie Foundation and the University of Virginia's Center for Alcohol & Substance Education. The Gordie Center, dedicated to the memory of Gordie Bailey, an 18-year-old freshman at the University of Colorado who died of alcohol poisoning after a fraternity hazing ritual in 2004, creates and distributes evidence-based educational programs and materials to reduce hazardous drinking and hazing and promote peer intervention among young adults.

Hank Nuwer – An author and professor who specializes in hazing education http://www.hanknuwer.com/

Haze, "The Movie" - http://gordiescall.org/haze-the-movie

In 2008, The Gordie Foundation produced HAZE, a documentary film telling Gordie's story and "connecting the dots" between college drinking and hazing. In the past four years, nearly 400 high schools, colleges and other organizations have purchased the full-length 82-minute) or abridged (36-minute) version to incorporate into their educational efforts.

Hazing Prevention: www.hazingprevention.org

HazingPrevention.Org is a group that is specifically dedicated to preventing hazing on college campuses. The organization started Hazing Prevention Week and has information on how on-campus organizations can get involved. Students can learn more about hazing and Hazing Prevention by reading their newsletters or participating in webinars through their website.

Inside Hazing - http://www.insidehazing.com/

MISSION: To provide methods of prevention and intervention in hazing; to explain the psychology of hazing in high school, college, the military and the workplace. Educational information is included for use in anti-hazing initiatives among fraternities, sororities, teams and other groups.

MASH – Mothers Against School Hazing: http://www.campushealthandsafety.org/resources/resource_rws_249.html

National Collaborative for Hazing Research and Prevention: www.hazingstudy.org

The NCHRP conducts research to provide evidence based hazing prevention and intervention strategies. This group believes that by sharing their research and educating people on hazing and its causes enables them to devise impactful prevention initiatives.

National Collegiate Athletic Association (NCAA): www.ncaa.org

This site has information for student athletes, administrators, and coaches in their hazing prevention efforts.

National Hazing Prevention Week: http://www.hazingprevention.org/about/mission.html

Mission: Empowering people to prevent hazing in college and university student groups.

Stop Hazing: Educating to Eliminate Hazing

www.stophazing.org StopHazing.org provides information for students, family members, and educators. The site includes hazing statistics, laws, myths/facts, and other related information for college campuses.

WiKipedia on Hazing - http://en.wikipedia.org/wiki/Hazing_in_Greek_letter_organizations

References

Allan, E. J. & Madden, M. (2008). *Hazing in view: College students at risk. Initial findings from the national study of student hazing.* Retrieved October 2, 2012, from World Wide Web: http://books.google.com/books?hl=en&lr=&id=L6A06KMi-28C&oi=fnd&pg=PA5&dq=Initial+Findings+from+the+National+Study+of+Student+Hazing:+Elizabeth+Allan&ots=igacxDc6Az&sig=DJ1FKyekeBxhvse2qTW03KZwOUg#v=onepage&q=Initial%20Findings%20from%20the%20National%20Study%20of%20Student%20Hazing%3A%20Elizabeth%20Allan&f=false

Alfred University (2012). *Hazing policy.* Retrieved October 2, 2012, from World Wide Web: http://my.alfred.edu/index.cfm/fuseaction/student_policies.hazing_0708.cfm

Burney, DeAnna M. (2012). "Psychological solutions for the elimination of hazing." Retrieved September 3, 2012, from World Wide Web: http://capitaloutlook.com/wordpress/?p=7205

Center for Advanced Research on Language Acquisition - CARLA (2012). *What is culture?* Retrieved November 2, 2012, from World Wide Web: http://www.carla.umn.edu/culture/definitions.html

Chang, Glenna C. "The hidden curriculum: Hazing and professional identify." Seattle Pacific University, 2011. United States—Washington: ProQuest Dissertations & Theses (PQDT); ProQuest Dissertations & Theses A&I. Web. 3 Oct. 2012.

Collins English Dictionary – Complete & Unabridged 10th Edition. Retrieved November 2, 2012, from Dictionary.com website: http://dictionary.reference.com/browse/socialization

Ellsworth, Chad Williams. "Definition of hazing: Differences among selected student organizations." University of Maryland, College Park, 2004. United States—Maryland: ProQuest Dissertations & Theses (PQDT); ProQuest Dissertations & Theses A&I. Web. 3 Oct. 2012.

Fraternal Information Programming Group. Definition. Retrieved November 2, 2012, from http://en.wikipedia.org/wiki/Hazing_in_Greek_letter_organizations

Gallagher and Graham (2005). National survey of counseling center directors. Retrieved October 3, 2012, from World Wide Web: http://www.collegecounseling.org/pdf/2005_survey.pdf

Galloway, J. (2012). Greek life rallies against the times. Retrieved November 2, 2012, from http://www.bupipedream.com/news/11895/greek-life-rallies/

Gayaden, Shashi Marion. "Social problems: Claimsmakers in the institutionalization of anti-hazing legislation." State University of New York at Buffalo, 2012. United States—New York: ProQuest Dissertations & Theses (PQDT); ProQuest Dissertations & Theses A&I. Web. 3 Oct. 2012.

Grant, J. H. (2012). "A position paper on the theological perspective of hazing." National Anti- hazing/Anti-Violence Conference at South Carolina State University, SC; and National

Newspaper Publishers Association Conference at Hilton Hotel, Richmond, VI.

Hightower Warren, P. (2012). "The sociological lens and the problem of hazing." Retrieved September 3, 2012, from World Wide Web: http://capitaloutlook.com/wordpress/?s=hazing%3A+Patricia+Warren+Hightower

Hughes, M.A. (2008). "Preventing college and university violence: A decision-maker's guide to implementing best practices." Alliant International University, San Diego, 2009. United States—

California: ProQuest Dissertations & Theses (PQDT); ProQuest Dissertations & Theses A&I. Web 3 Oct. 2012.

Hoover, N.C. (1999). *National Survey: Initiation rites and athletics for NCAA sports teams.* Retrieved October 2, 2012, from World Wide Web: http://www.alfred.edu/sports_hazing/docs/hazing.pdf

Hoover, N.C., Pollard, N.J., (2000). *Intiation rites in American high schools: A national survey.* Retrived October 2, 2012, from World Wide Web: http://www.alfred.edu/hs_hazing/

Keating, C.F., Pomerantz, J., Pommer, S.D., Ritt, S.J., Miller, L.H., & McCormick, J. (2005). Going to college and unpacking hazing: A functional approach to decrypting initiation practice among undergraduates. *Group Dynamics: Theory, Research, and Practice, 9,* 104 – 126.

Lipkins, S. (2006). *Preventing Hazing: How parents, teachers, and coaches can stop the violence, harassment, and humiliation.*

Lyons, J.N. (2012). "Hazing is a choice…and a crime." Retrieved September 3, 2012, from World Wide Web: http://capitaloutlook.com/wordpress/?p=6992

National Institute of Mental Health (2007). *The number count: Mental disorders in America.* Retrieved October 3, 2012, from World Wide Web: http://www.nimh.nih.gov/health/publications/the-numbers-count-mental-disorders-in-america/index.shtml

Nuwer, H. (1990). *Broken pledges: The deadly rites of hazing.* Atlanta, GA: Longstreet Press.

Nuwer, H. (1999). *Wrong of passage: Fraternities, sororities, hazing, and binge drinking.* Bloomington: Indiana University Press.

Nuwer, H. (2004). *The hazing reader.* Bloomington: Indiana University Press.

NCAA (2007). *Building new traditions: Hazing prevention in college athletics.* Retrieved October 3, 2012, from World Wide Web: http://

counseling.sdes.ucf.edu/docs/hazinghandbook0108%5B1%5D. pdf

Nuwer, H. (revised ed. 2001). "A weed in the garden of academe. Retrieved October 2, 2012, from World Wide Web: http://www. hanknuwer.com/hazingdeaths.html

Reisberg, L. (1999). Court says U. of Nebraska had duty to protect pledge from hazing. <u>The Chronicle of Higher Education, 11, 1-2.</u>

Rogers, I.H. (2012). Commentary: Hazing and American culture. Retrieved November 2, 2012, from World Wide Web: http:// diverseeducation.com/article/48127/

Substance Abuse & Mental Health Services Administration (2007). Results from the 2007 national survey on drug use and health: National findings. Retrieved October 3, 2012, from World Wide Web: http://www.samhsa.gov/data/nsduh/2k7nsduh/2k7Results.htm

StopHazing.org. Educating to eliminate hazing. Retrieved October 3, 2012, from World Wide Web: http://www.stophazing.org/ mythsandfacts.html

Swigert, Lance Patrick. "An exploratory study of safe initiation activities and trainings offered to Greek Letter Organizations at Land Grant Universities." Oklahoma State University, College, 2005. United States—Oklahoma City: Proquest Dissertations & Theses (PQDT); ProQuest Dissertations & Theses A&I. Web. 3 Oct. 2012.

Winter, M. (2011). Death of hazed FAMU drum major ruled homicide. Retrieved October 3, 2012, from World Wide Web: http:// content.usatoday.com/communities/ondeadline/post/2011/12/ death-of-famu-drum-major-ruled-homicide/1#.UIg9S83oJD4

Author's Background

Ronald Holmes is the author of two books: "Education Questions to be Answered" and "Current Issues and Answers in Education." He is the sponsoring editor for the landmark book, "Surviving and Thriving: Candid, Real Life Stories of Prostate Cancer."

Ronald Holmes is president and publisher of The Holmes Education Post, an education focused Internet newspaper. His philanthropist spirit and unselfish giving has enabled him to provide free educational resources and publications to educators across the nation. He publishes weekly articles on educational issues and offers unique, researched based solutions, perspectives, best practices and resources to improve public education.

Ronald Holmes is a member of the National Association of School Superintendents, national superintendent of the National Save the Family Now Movement, Inc. and vice president and education editor of Live Communications, Inc. (Capital Outlook Newspaper and WTAL 1450 AM). He earned a Ph.D. in Educational Leadership, a ME.D. in Educational Administration and Supervision and a B.S. in Business Education from Florida A&M University. He also earned a ME.D. in Business Education from Bowling Green State University. He has proven success working from the elementary to the collegiate level.

Ronald Holmes is a native of Jacksonville, Florida and married to Constance Holmes. He is an avid jogger and enjoys competitive races.